CHEMICAL PROCESS AND EQUIPMENT DESIGN

K. A. GAVHANE
Vice-Principal & Head of Chemical Engg. Dept.
S.E. Society's Satara Polytechnic,
Satara.

NIRALI ™
PRAKASHAN
ADVANCEMENT OF KNOWLEDGE

N0905

CHEMICAL PROCESS AND EQUIPMENT DESIGN

ISBN 978-93-81237-05-2

Sixth Edition	:	March 2019
©	:	Authors

Published By :

NIRALI PRAKASHAN

Abhyudaya Pragati, 1312, Shivaji Nagar
Off J.M. Road, Pune – 411005
Tel - (020) 25512336/37/39, Fax - (020) 25511379
Email : niralipune@pragationline.com

➢ DISTRIBUTION CENTRES

PUNE

Nirali Prakashan : 119, Budhwar Peth, Jogeshwari Mandir Lane, Pune 411002, Maharashtra
(For orders within Pune) Tel : (020) 2445 2044, 66022708, Fax : (020) 2445 1538; Mobile : 9657703145
Email : niralilocal@pragationline.com

Nirali Prakashan : S. No. 28/27, Dhayari, Near Asian College Pune 411041
(For orders outside Pune) Tel : (020) 24690204 Fax : (020) 24690316; Mobile : 9657703143
Email : bookorder@pragationline.com

MUMBAI

Nirali Prakashan : 385, S.V.P. Road, Rasdhara Co-op. Hsg. Society Ltd.,
Girgaum, Mumbai 400004, Maharashtra; Mobile : 9320129587
Tel : (022) 2385 6339 / 2386 9976, Fax : (022) 2386 9976
Email : niralimumbai@pragationline.com

➢ DISTRIBUTION BRANCHES

JALGAON

Nirali Prakashan : 34, V. V. Golani Market, Navi Peth, Jalgaon 425001, Maharashtra,
Tel : (0257) 222 0395, Mob : 94234 91860; Email : niralijalgaon@pragationline.com

KOLHAPUR

Nirali Prakashan : New Mahadvar Road, Kedar Plaza, 1st Floor Opp. IDBI Bank, Kolhapur 416 012
Maharashtra. Mob : 9850046155; Email : niralikolhapur@pragationline.com

NAGPUR

Nirali Prakashan : Above Maratha Mandir, Shop No. 3, First Floor,
Rani Jhanshi Square, Sitabuldi, Nagpur 440012, Maharashtra
Tel : (0712) 254 7129; Email : niralinagpur@pragationline.com

DELHI

Nirali Prakashan : 4593/15, Basement, Agarwal Lane, Ansari Road, Daryaganj
Near Times of India Building, New Delhi 110002 Mob : 08505972553
Email : niralidelhi@pragationline.com

BENGALURU

Nirali Prakashan : Maitri Ground Floor, Jaya Apartments, No. 99, 6th Cross, 6th Main,
Malleswaram, Bengaluru 560003, Karnataka; Mob : 9449043034
Email: niralibangalore@pragationline.com

Other Branches : Hyderabad, Chennai

niralipune@pragationline.com | www.pragationline.com

Also find us on ⓕ www.facebook.com/niralibooks

PREFACE TO THE FIFTH EDITION

I am very happy to present the fifth edition of the book **Chemical Process and Equipment Design** to the students of Chemical Engineering.

The matter is arranged in a proper sequence, written in a simple and lucid language, with simplified diagrams, so as to grasp it very easily.

I am very thankful to the publisher Shri D. K. Furia, Shri Jignesh Furia and the staff of Nirali Prakashan for the timely publication of the book.

I will be glad to receive suggestions regarding improvement of the book.

I hope that the students will appreciate the content of the book.

K.A. Gavhane
Mobile : 9850242440

PREFACE TO THE FIRST EDITION

The operations involving physical changes – **Chemical Process and Equipment Design** are commonly encountered in every chemical and process industry.

The text **Chemical Process and Equipment Design** is prepared as per the syllabus for students of Third Year Diploma in Chemical Engineering. The matter is arranged in a proper sequence with simplified diagrams to grasp it very easily by students of in chemical engineering/technology. The students of degree chemical engineering/technology will also find the matter very helpful.

I am very thankful to the publisher Shri. D. K. Furia, Jignesh Furia for pursuing me to complete this book.

I hope that the students will appreciate the content of the book.

K.A. Gavhane
Mobile : 9850242440

SYLLABUS AND CONTENTS

•••

FLOW SHEET SYMBOLS - IS 3232

The process flow sheets are to be drawn by making use of flow sheet symbols (graphical symbols) for the equipments, transportation devices, etc. that are involved in a given process. To reduce the detailed description on the flow sheets, it is usual practice to develop or adopt a set of symbols. A symbol should have a fairly close resemblance to the actual equipment involved. For symbolic representation of equipments, etc., the symbols given in Indian standard 3232-1976 [IS : 3232-1976] that were adopted by the Indian Standards Institution on 29/11/1976 are listed below.

One should note that the units symbolised here may or may not be provided with required inlets and outlets or means of connection to other units. Additional inlet, outlet or connection lines are to be shown in the flow sheets or flow diagrams. Whenever required two or more of these basic symbols may be combined to represent composite units. Please note that in the flow diagrams, one has to draw the symbols neatly and proportionately to represent the equipments under consideration.

1.1 REACTORS

Sr. No.	Description	Symbol	Sr. No.	Description	Symbol
1.1.1	Batch reactor (jacketed)		1.1.2	Batch reactor (with cooling coil)	
1.1.3	Batch reactor (with jacket as well as coil)		1.1.4	CSTR (jacketed)	
1.1.5	CSTR (with coil)		1.1.6	Semibatch reactor	Same as batch reactor
1.1.7	Fixed bed reactor (catalytic reactor)	IS - 3232 - 1976	1.1.8	Fixed bed reactor (catalytic reactor) may be preferred	IS - 3232 - 1965
1.1.9	Fluidised bed		1.1.10	Fluidised bed reactor	

1.1.11	Autoclave				

1.2 SIZE REDUCTION EQUIPMENTS

Sr. No.	Description	Symbol	Sr. No.	Description	Symbol
1.2.1	Size reducing equipment (general symbol) e.g. pulverizer		1.2.2	Breaker, gyratory	
1.2.3	Breaker, hammer mill, impact mill		1.2.4	Jaw crusher	
1.2.5	Roller crusher		1.2.6	Grinder	
1.2.7	Ball or tube mill				

1.3 FILTERS

Sr. No.	Description	Symbol	Sr. No.	Description	Symbol
1.3.1	Filter press		1.3.2	Suction filter	
1.3.3	Pressure filter		1.3.4	Gravity filter (open settling tank)	
1.3.5	Open rotary vacuum filter		1.3.6	Closed rotary vacuum filter	
1.3.7	Bag filter				

1.4 DRIERS

Sr. No.	Description	Symbol	Sr. No.	Description	Symbol
1.4.1	Batch tray drier		1.4.2	Spray drier	

1.4.3	Continuous drier		1.4.4	Rotary drier or kiln	
1.4.5	Drum drier or flaker				

1.5 DIFFERENT TYPES OF COLUMNS

Sr. No.	Description	Symbol	Sr. No.	Description	Symbol
1.5.1	Plate column (tower) for distillation etc.		1.5.2	Packed column (tower), packed vessel, absorber or scrubber	
1.5.3	Fixed bed packed column (for distillation)		1.5.4	Column (tower) sectioned	
1.5.5	Spray column IS-3232-1965	IS - 3232 - 1965			

1.6 STORAGE VESSELS

Sr. No.	Description	Symbol	Sr. No.	Description	Symbol
1.6.1	Storage tank, fixed roof		1.6.2	Storage tank, floating roof	
1.6.3	Gas holder, water seal		1.6.4	Gas holder, dry seal	
1.6.5	Pressure storage (sphere or spheroid)		1.6.6	Gas cylinder	

1.7 HEAT EXCHANGERS

Sr. No.	Description	Symbol	Sr. No.	Description	Symbol
1.7.1	Heat exchanger	OR	1.7.2	Plate heat exchanger (IS - 3232-1965)	IS - 3232 - 1965

1.8 PUMPS AND COMPRESSORS

Sr. No.	Description	Symbol	Sr. No.	Description	Symbol
1.8.1	Centrifugal pump		1.8.2	Positive displacement pump (reciprocating pump, gear pump)	

1.8.3	Rotary pump (screw pump) IS-3232-1965		1.8.4	Proportioning or metering pump	
1.8.5	Blowing egg blow egg		1.8.6	Ejector pump	
1.8.7	Centrifugal compressor		1.8.8	Positive displacement compressor	
1.8.9	Fan		1.8.10	Ejector compressor	
1.8.11	Turbine		1.8.12	Blower centrifugal IS-3232-1965	

1.9 MATERIAL HANDLING

Sr. No.	Description	Symbol	Sr. No.	Description	Symbol
1.9.1	Feeder (General symbol)		1.9.2	Vibrator feeder	
1.9.3	Weigh feeder		1.9.4	Rotary table feeder, revolving plate feeder	
1.9.5	Scraper feeder		1.9.6	Screw feeder	
1.9.7	Rotary feeder		1.9.8	Belt conveyor	
1.9.9	Scraper conveyor		1.9.10	Vibrating conveyor	
1.9.11	Screw conveyor		1.9.12	Bucket or flight conveyor or elevator	
1.9.13	Roller conveyor		1.9.14	Overhead conveyor with hooks	

1.9.15	Overhead conveyor or ropeway with buckets or carriers		1.9.16	Fixed hoist with hook	
1.9.17	Travelling hoist with hook		1.9.18	Travelling hoist with grab	
1.9.19	Transport vehicle, ship		1.9.20	Wagon, lorry	
1.9.21	Tanker		1.9.22	Open trailer	
1.9.23	Wagon-bottom hopper				

1.10 STRAINERS

Sr. No.	Description	Symbol
1.10.1	Strainer	

1.11 VALVES

Sr. No.	Description	Symbol	Sr. No.	Description	Symbol
1.11.1	Valve (General symbol)		1.11.2	Valve specific (insert code letter in the box)	
1.11.3	Gate valve		1.11.4	Globe valve	
1.11.5	Diaphragm valve		1.11.6	Plug cock/plug valve	
1.11.7	Butterfly valve		1.11.8	Needle valve	
1.11.9	Check or non-return valve		1.11.10	Ball valve IS-9446-1980 (Preferred)	
1.11.11	Gate valve IS-9446-1980		1.11.12	Globe valve (Preferred) IS-9446-1980	

1.11.13	Diaphragm valve IS-9446		1.11.14	Foot valve IS - 9446	
1.11.15	Control valve IS-9446		1.11.16	Plug valve IS-9446 (Preferred)	
1.11.17	Solenoid valve (two way)		1.11.18	Solenoid valve (three way)	
1.11.19	Angle valve		1.11.20	Three way cock	
1.11.21	Float operating valve		1.11.22	Butterfly valve (IS-9446)	

1.12 TEMPERATURE, PRESSURE, LEVEL INDICATORS AND CONTROLLERS (INSTRUMENTATION SYMBOLS)

Sr. No.	Description	Symbol	Sr. No.	Description	Symbol
1.12.1	Instrument air signal IS-9446-1980		1.12.2	Instrument electric leads	
1.12.3	Instrument capillary tubing		1.12.4	Hydraulic lines	
1.12.5	Locally mounted instruments		1.12.6	Instrument (main panel mounted)	
1.12.7	Instrument (mounted-local panel)		1.12.8	Transmeter, locally mounted	
1.12.9	Transmeter, panel mounted		1.12.10	Instrument-ation identification	
1.12.11	Unit (plant) No. 9, pressure indicator and controller, locally mounted, instrument No. 100		1.12.12	Level indicator and controller, panel mounted, instrument No. 90	

1.12.13 Process variable symbols

1.12.13.1	Ratio	r	1.12.13.2	Pressure	P
1.12.13.3	Temperature	T	1.12.13.4	Flow	F
1.12.13.5	Level	L	1.12.13.6	Density	D
1.12.13.7	Concentration / quality	Q	1.12.13.8	Viscosity	V
1.12.13.9	H_2 ion concentration	pH	1.12.13.10	Speed	S

1.12.14 Instrument function symbols

1.12.14.1	Indicator	I	1.12.14.2	Controller	C
1.12.14.3	Recorder	R	1.12.14.4	Gauge	G
1.12.14.5	Alarms	A			

1.13 SAFETY VALVES

1.13.1	Pressure relief or safety valve	
1.14	**Rupture disc / burst disc**	
1.15	**Vent**	
1.16	**Tundish / drain funnel**	
1.17	**Steam trap**	IS - 9446
1.18 Weighing systems/machines		
1.18.1	Basic	
1.18.2	Weighbridge	
1.18.3	Tank weigher	
1.19 Vacuum relief valve		
1.20 Flame arrester		

1.21 Flare	
1.22 Chimney	
1.23 Sight flow indicator	
1.24 Pipe line	
1.24.1 Inflow line (For Main Raw Materials)	
1.24.2 Outflow line (For desired product)	
1.24.3 Connecting line	
1.24.4 Cross over line	
1.24.5 Direction of process line	
1.24.6 Dead end	
1.24.7 Tracer line	
1.24.8 Jacketed pipe	
1.24.9 Hose coupling	
1.24.10 Change of pipe size	
1.24.11 Insulation	
1.24.12 Insulated pipe	
1.25 Insulated equipment	
1.26 Process quantities	
1.26.1 Liquid flow	(Place value inside)
1.26.2 Gas flow	(Place value inside)

1.26.3	Pressure and temperature	ATM/kPa °C (Place value inside)
1.27	**Sight glass (IS-9446)**	SG
1.28	**Rotameter (IS-9446)**	
1.29	**Orifice**	
1.30	**Venturi**	
1.31	**Immersion coil (Heating and cooling)**	
1.32	**Jacket**	
1.33	**Tubular coil**	
1.34	**Evaporator**	
1.35	**Crystalliser**	
1.36	**Stirrer**	
1.37	**Sparger**	

1.38 Centrifuges

1.38.1	Centrifuges (General symbol)		1.38.2	Basket centrifuge, batch or continuous	

1.38.3	Plate centrifuge				
1.39	Pneumatic conveyor (IS-3232-1965)				

1.40 Process vessels

1.40.1	Horizontal drum		1.40.2	Vertical drum	

1.41 Furnaces, boilers and burners

1.41.1	Burner (basic) (Alternative)		1.41.2	Solid fuel furnace	
1.41.3	Oil, gas or pulverised fuel furnace		1.41.4	Electrical furnace	
1.41.5	Fired boiler		1.41.6	Waste heat boiler	
1.42	Plate type heat exchanger				

1.43 Separators

1.43.1	Cyclone or hydrocyclone		1.43.2	Electrostatic separator	
1.43.3	Separators for liquids, decantors	or	1.43.4	Thickener	

1.44 Screens

1.44.1	Screen, vibratory		1.44.2	Screen, rotary	

1.45 Mixers

1.45.1	Kneader		1.45.2	Ribbon blender	
1.45.3	Double cone blender		1.45.4	Rotary mixer	
1.45.5	In-line mixer		1.45.6	Ejector mixer	
1.46	Jacketed vessel (kettle type)		1.47	Induced draught cooling tower	
1.48	Forced draught cooling tower		1.49	Contact condenser	
1.50	Trickle cooler		1.51	Nuclear reactor (IS-3232-1965)	
1.52	Centrifugal separator (IS-3232-1965)		1.53	Boiler (thermo-syphon) Reboiler (thermo-syphon) (IS-3232-1965)	
1.54	Kettle type reboiler		1.55	Vaporiser	
1.56	Fluidised bed dryer		1.57	Cooler	
1.58	Air cooler		1.59	Condenser	

1.60	Double pipe heat exchanger		1.61	Air preheater	
1.62	Half coil jacket		1.63	Finned tube heat exchanger	
1.64	Decanter (with surge chamber)		1.65	Oil cooler	
1.66	Heater				

This chapter lists symbols cited in IS-3232-1976. Some of the symbols not available in IS-3232-1976 are taken from IS-3232-1965 (though it is outdated). The use of standard symbols as per IS-3232-1976 is recommended. For valves though symbols as per IS-3232-1976 are available, the use of symbols as per IS-9446-1980 is recommended as the symbols as per IS-9446-1980 are seem to be more convenient. For some equipments, symbols in IS-3232-1976 are not available, so for such equipments, the symbols from sources are taken and used.

❐❐❐

VALVES

A valve is a mechanical device used either to regulate the flow/control flow or to stop the flow of a fluid through a pipe line or in or out of a vessel. Valves, in addition to regulate the flow, serve to isolate piping or equipment for maintenance without interrupting other connected equipments. Valves in common have a flow regulating element called a plug (valve plug) and it rests on a seat (valve seat) in the valve body. The ends of the valves may be threaded or flanged but in industry flanged valves are very common. The valves may be operated by the pressure of the fluid (self operating) or by hand (operated manually) or by some external mechanism (operated by means of air pressure).

In the chemical industry, various types of valves are used depending upon the process conditions/requirements and fluids to be handled. The various types of valves used in the chemical industry are :

(i) Gave valve, (ii) Globe valve, (iii) Ball valve, (iv) Non-return valve, (v) Needle valve, (vi) Plug valve, (vii) Butterfly valve, (viii) Diaphram valve, (ix) Control valve (pneumatically operated), (x) Safety valve (pressure relief valve), (xi) Pressure reducing valve and (xii) Solenoid valve. Gate, plug and ball valves are shut-off valves whose purpose is to close-off the flow and not to regulate flow.

2.1 GATE VALVES

Gate valves are used for minimising the pressure drop in open position. These valves are used primarily for on-off applications. Gate valves are suited for high pressure and high temperature use with wide variety of fluids. They are not suited for slurries and viscous fluids.

A gate valve is a valve that provides a straight through passage for the flow of a fluid. A gate is moved up and down within a body by a stem whose axis is at right angles to that of the body ends. In gate valves, the diameter of the opening through which the fluid passes is nearly the same as that of the pipe. In these valves, the direction of flow does not change and as a result the pressure drop through them is very low in fully open condition. Therefore, gate valves are used to minimise pressure drop in the open position and to stop the flow instead of to regulate the flow of fluid.

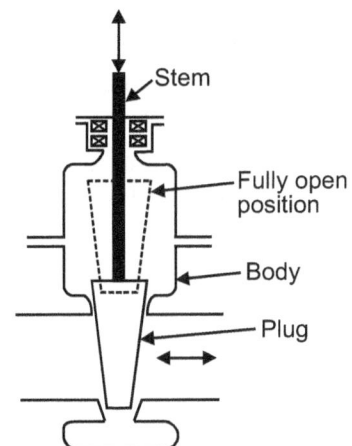

Fig. 2.1 : Gate valve

2.2 GLOBE VALVES

A globe valve is used to control/regulate the flow of fluid. It is the most commonly used valve for efficient regulation of a critical service. Used extensively for automatic process control and for high temperature applications. These valves are not normally used for on-off service.

A globe valve is a valve having generally a spherical body in which the axis of a stem is at right angles to that of the body ends. Pressure drop through globe valves is much greater than that for gate valves due to change in the direction of fluid flow.

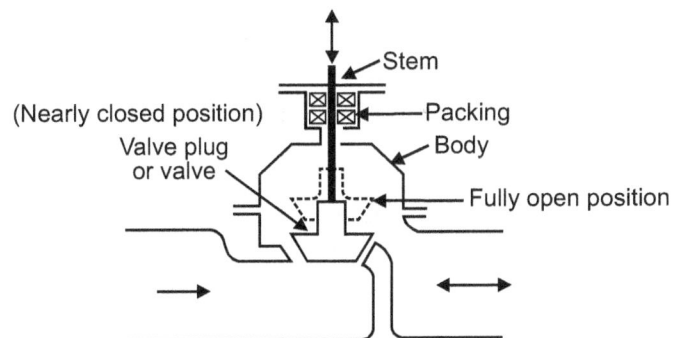

Fig. 2.2 : Globe valve

2.3 BALL VALVES

It is used for flow control and on-off service. Widely used in industry where conditions of corrosion plus temperature/pressure exist. These valves are simple, compact and quick opening and they are operated through 90°. They are good for conditions which require to be fire safe. They are constructed in a very wide size and temperature – pressure ranges. These valves are used for corrosive liquids, cryogenic liquids and gases.

It is a valve in which a spherical closure element (ball) having a port through it (passage) is turned substantially through 90° from close to open position.

Easy to maintain, tight shut-off, quarter turn operation, quick operating and low pressure drop.

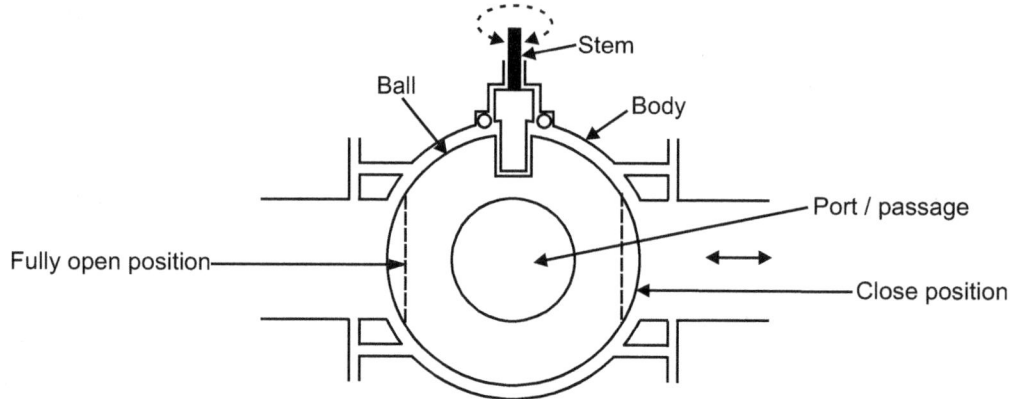

Fig. 2.3 : Ball valve free ball

2.4 CHECK VALVES

These valves are used when unidirection flow is desired. Automatically prevents reversal of flow/automatically prevents the flow of the fluid in the reverse direction
(i.e., backflow) in lines. Available in wide sizes and temperature/pressure ranges. It can be mounted in a horizontal or vertical line.

It is a valve that prevents reversal of flow by means of a check mechanism, the valve being opened by the pressure of the flowing fluid and closed by weight of the check mechanism when the flow ceases or by back pressure. These are also called non-return valves.

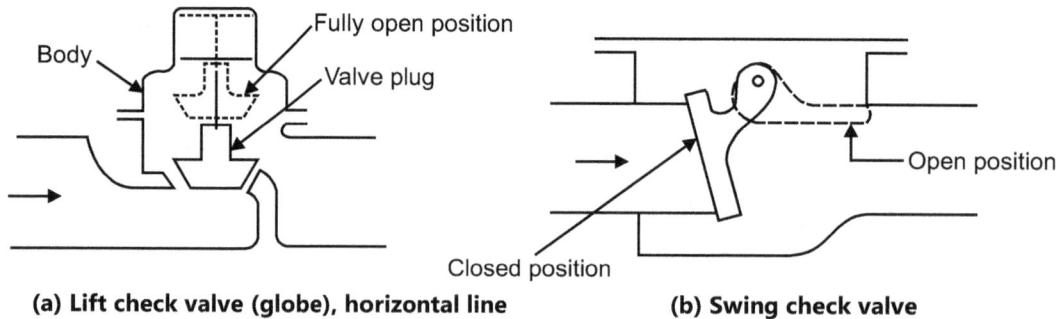

(a) Lift check valve (globe), horizontal line   **(b) Swing check valve**

Vertical lift check valves are used in vertical lines where the flow is normally upward. Globe check valves are used in horizontal lines.

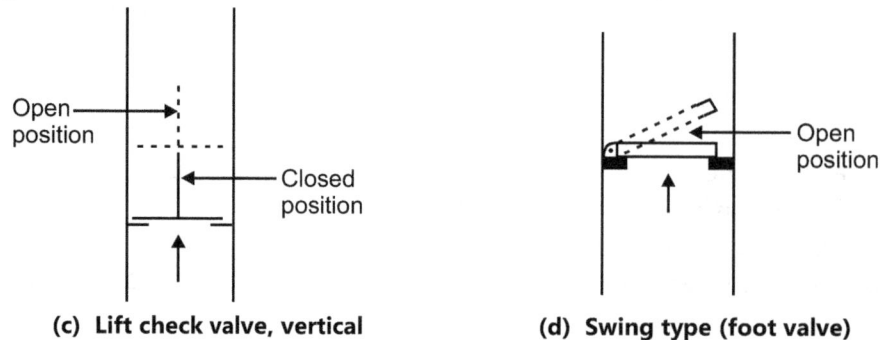

(c) Lift check valve, vertical   **(d) Swing type (foot valve)**

Fig. 2.4

2.5 DIAPHRAM VALVES

It is a glandless type of valve used for corrosive, volatile and toxic fluids particularly where leakage must be avoided. They are also suited for handling slurries. They are used for regulating the flow and also for on-off service. These valves may be installed in any position.

A diaphram valve is a valve that contains a flexible rubber (natural or synthetic) diaphram as a plug.

In this valve, the diaphram (usually of rubber) keeps the working parts in isolation from the process liquid. The lined bodies act as an in-built gasket for the connecting flanges. These valves are constructed out of plastics or metals (rubber lined).

Butterfly valves are used for the control of gas and vapour flows.

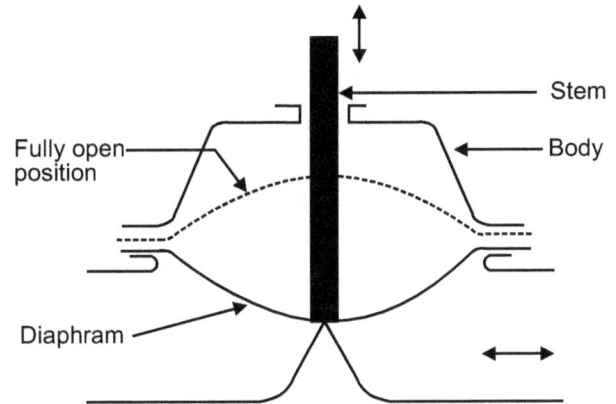

Fig. 2.5 : Diaphram valve

2.6 BUTTERFLY VALVES

These valves are specially suited for large flow of gases, liquids, and slurries at low pressures. Suited for throttling as well as on-off services and offer low pressure drop. It is extremely simple in construction, quick opening, low weight and low priced.

It has a disk-shaped closure element that rotates about a central shaft (stem).

It is a valve in which the disk is turned substantially through 90° from close to open position, on an axis right angles to that of the valve ports.

These valves occupy less space in the line than any other valves.

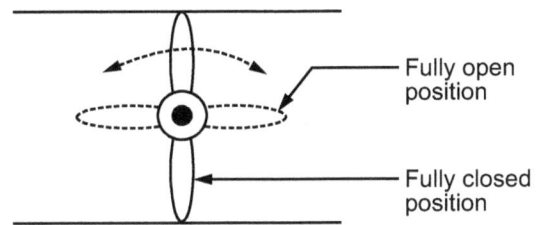

Fig. 2.6 : Butterfly valve

2.7 PLUG VALVES

Straight-through flow, positive shut-off, quarter turn operation-open to close, used for multiport operation (i.e., 2, 3, and 4 way), hence simplifying piping system. Used for general on-off service.

It is a form of shut-off device comprising a body with a parallel or taper cylindrical seating into which a plug is fitted which may be turned to move its port(s) relative to the body seat ports to control the flow of fluid. As it is operated through 90° with the help of a handle, it is easily opened and closed. Used for water lines (cooling tower water, chilled water).

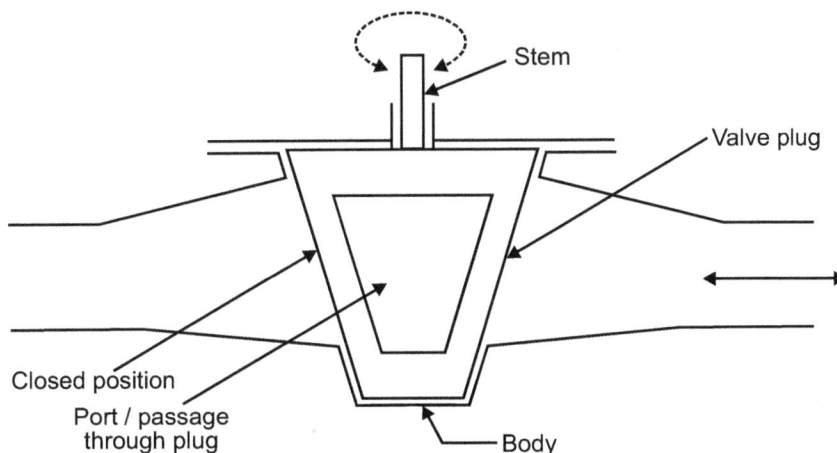

Fig. 2.7 : Plug valve

Control Valves :

In automatic process control systems, the most commonly used final control element is a diaphram motor valve. It consists of a pneumatic diaphram motor actuator and a process fluid control valve. The actuator positions the valve plug in the orifice in response to a signal from the automatic controller. The valve operated pneumatically may be air to open or air to close type.

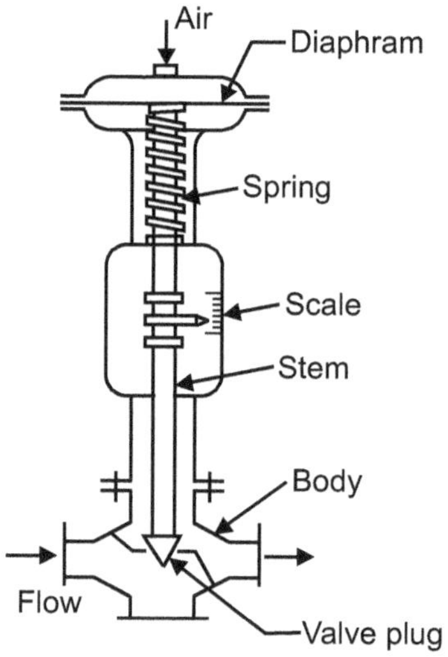

Fig. 2.8 : Control valve

Table 2.1 : Recommended valve services [indicative]

Valve	On-off	Throttling	Frequent operation	Low press drop	Slurry handling	Quick opening	Free draining	Prevent reversal of flow	Prevent over pressure
Gate	X	–	–	X	–	X	X	–	–
Globe	X	X	X	–	–	–	–	–	–
Ball	X	X	X	X	–	X	–	–	–
Plug	X	X	X	X	–	X	X	–	–
Butterfly	X	X	X	X	X	X	X	–	–
Diaphram	X	X	–	–	X	X	X	–	–
Swing check	–	–	–	X	–	–	–	X	–
Lift check	–	–	–	–	–	–	–	X	–
Foot valve	–	–	–	–	–	–	–	X	–
Pressure reducing	–	–	–	–	–	–	–	–	X
Pressure relief/safety valve	X	–	–	–	–	–	–	–	X

●●●

PIPE JOINTS

3.1 THREADED, FLANGED AND OTHER JOINTS

To carry fluids from one place to another, pipes are used. Pipes (long hollow cylinders with thin walls) are available in market in a wide range of materials of construction such as cast iron, mild steel, stainless steel, lead, etc. The selection of a suitable material of construction for the pipe line depends on the process conditions such as temperature, pressure and the corrosive nature of the fluid to be handled. Pipes are available in standard lengths and when we have to connect one process equipment to another, the transfer line consists of pipes of different lengths which are connected by variety joints depending upon the material of the pipes and the purpose for which they are used.

Two pieces of pipe may be joined by – welded joint, screwed joint or flanged joint.

Welded joints : The most widely used joint to join two pieces of pipe in piping practice is the butt-weld joint. Branch welds eliminate the need of purchase of pipe fittings such as tees and require no more weld metal than tees (Refer Fig. 3.1).

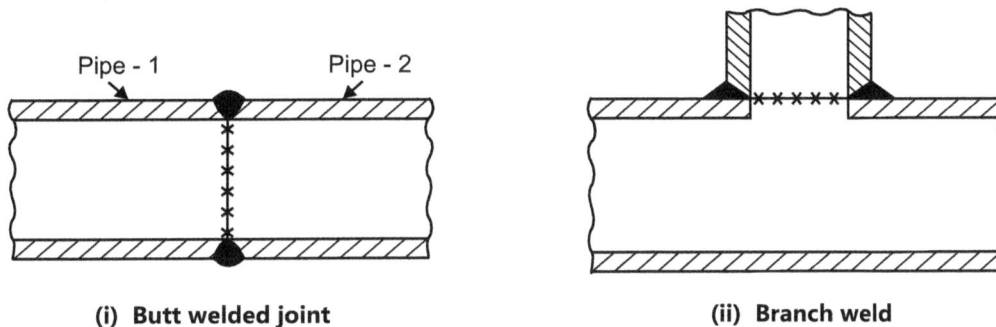

(i) Butt welded joint   **(ii) Branch weld**

Fig. 3.1 : Welded joints

Screwed / Threaded Joints :

Threaded joints are used especially for pipes having sizes 50 mm or smaller. Due to economic consideration, threaded joints for pipe above 50 mm are not recommended. In this case, the pipes to be joined are threaded on their ends and joined together by means of a suitable pipe fitting (Refer Fig. 3.2). Common methods for joining wrought iron and steel pipes are screwed joints and flanged joints. The wrought iron pipes are generally used for domestic purposes and galvanised all over.

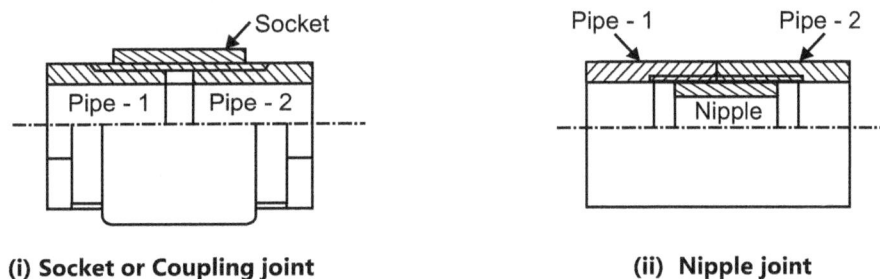

(i) Socket or Coupling joint   **(ii) Nipple joint**

Fig. 3.2 : Screwed joint

Flanged Joints :

In the chemical industry, a large majority of pipes are connected to each other as well as piping and nozzle connections to and from process equipments are connected to each other by flanged joints. Flanged joints are detachable type of joints. Flanged joints are most widely used for pipe size larger than two inch where disassembly is expected. Flanges are circular or oval shaped, and may be separate pieces or integral with the pipe end. Flanges are thick as compared to pieces or parts to be connected. To have a perfect joint, the flange faces must be machined accurately. Flanges are clamped with the help of nuts and bolts. For leakproof joints, gaskets are used between flange facings. (Refer to Fig. 3.17).

Fittings : The most common material of which fittings are made is gray cast iron. Where vibration is serious and there is a danger of cast iron cracking, malleable iron may be used. For high pressures or severe services, cast steel fittings are available and for exceptional cases, fittings forged from mild steel are available. The fittings may be threaded/screwed or flanged. For pipe sizes greater than two inch, screw fittings are less frequently encountered. Large size pipes can be joined by the same type of fittings, but it is usual to install flanged fittings.

3.2 BEND : SHORT AND LONG

Bends are used to change the direction of fluid flow. They are having external threads. The frictional losses in bends are small compared to those in elboows due to smooth change in the direction of flow.

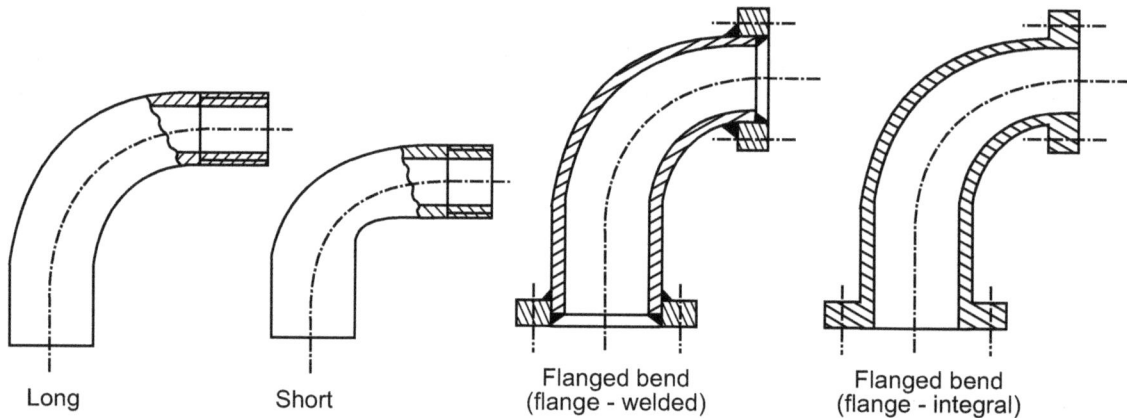

Long   Short   Flanged bend (flange - welded)   Flanged bend (flange - integral)

Fig. 3.3 : Bends

3.3 ELBOW

Elbows are used to change the direction of fluid flow. There is sudden change in the direction of flow and therefore, pressure drop is more in elbows than in bends.

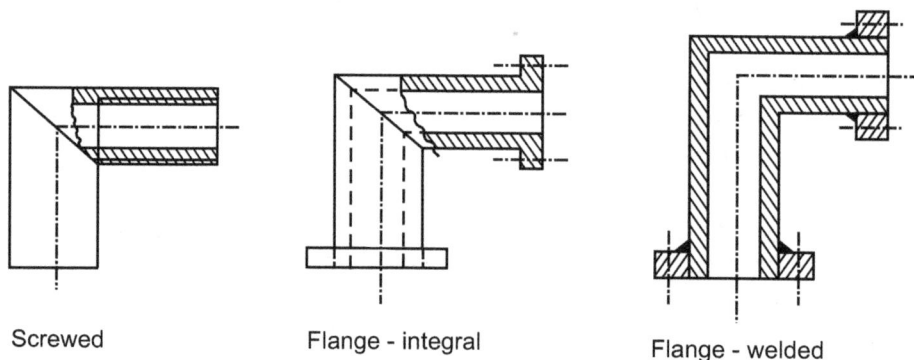

Screwed   Flange - integral   Flange - welded

Fig. 3.4 : Elbow

3.4 TEE

Pipes are branched off at right angles by means of fittings such as tees. Tees are having internal threads.

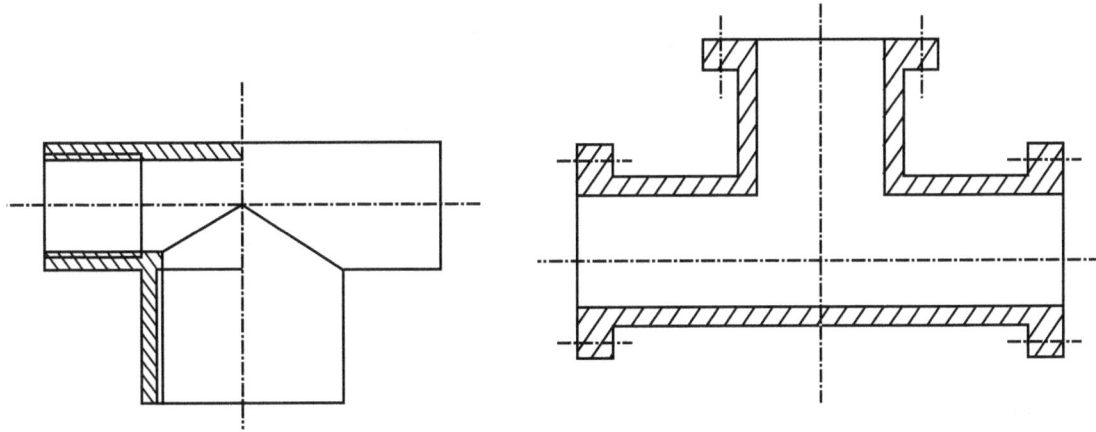

Fig. 3.5 : Tee

3.5 NIPPLE

It is a small piece of pipe with external threads throughout (i.e., threaded on the outside). It is screwed into the internally threaded ends of the pipes to be connected. It is used to join two pieces of pipe. In case of bare nipple there are threads only at the ends of small pipe piece (a bare nipple is a piece of pipe of length 75 mm, 100 mm, 150 mm, etc. having threads at the ends).

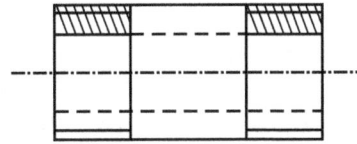

Fig. 3.6 : Nipple   **Fig. 3.7 : Bare nipple**

3.6 SOCKET

A socket also called as a coupler is used to join two pieces of pipe with their axes in alignment. It is a small piece of pipe with internal threads throughout. The socket is screwed on half way on the threaded end of one pipe and then the end of the other pipe is screwed into the socket in the remaining half.

Fig. 3.8 : Socket

3.7 REDUCING SOCKET (REDUCER)

To change the size of the pipe in a straight run (i.e., for changing the diameter of the pipe line) a reducer is used. Reducers are having internal threads.

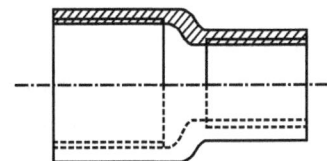

Fig. 3.9 : Reducing socket

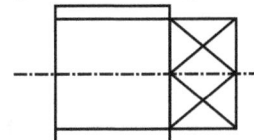

3.8 PLUG

These are used to close a pipe line at the end (for the termination of a pipe line). These are having external threads and provided with square heads.

Fig. 3.10 : Plug

3.9 UNION JOINT

In case of long piping, piping fixed to walls etc. to disengage the pipes they are joined by means of a union joint (union). In the case of union joint, pipes are disengaged by simply unscrewing a coupler nut.

This joint is formed by NUT-1 having internal as well as external threads (in which the end of one pipe is screwed), NUT-2 having only internal threads (in which the end of the other pipe is screwed) and NUT-3 (the coupler nut) which brings two pipes close together. A packing ring is inserted between the ends of two pipes to have a leakproof joint.

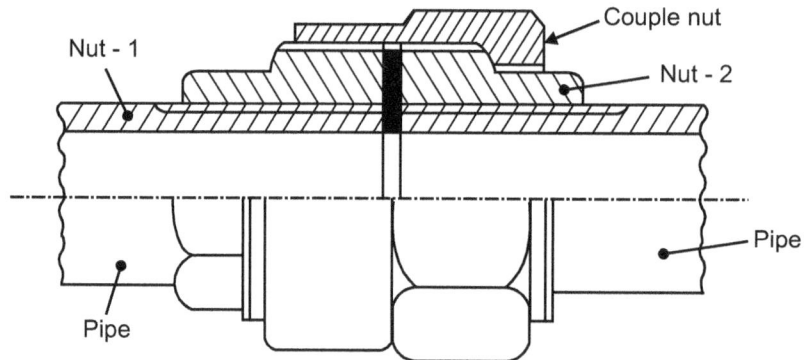

Fig. 3.11 : Union joint

3.10 BLIND FLANGES

These flanges are used to blank-off pressure vessel openings such as hand holes, man holes nozzles, inspection ports and to block off/close the ends of piping and valves.

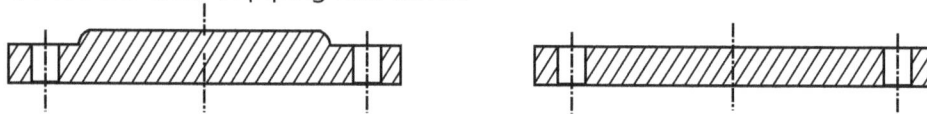

Fig. 3.12 : Blind flanges

3.11 SOCKET AND SPIGOT JOINT

This type of joint is used to connect underground cast iron pipes of very large diameters, e.g., cast-iron water supply piping. The spigot-end of one pipe is inserted and fits into the socket-end of the other pipe (Refer Fig. 3.13). A leakproof joint is achieved by filling the gap between the socket and spigot ends with several turns of jute yarn and finally pouring molten lead.

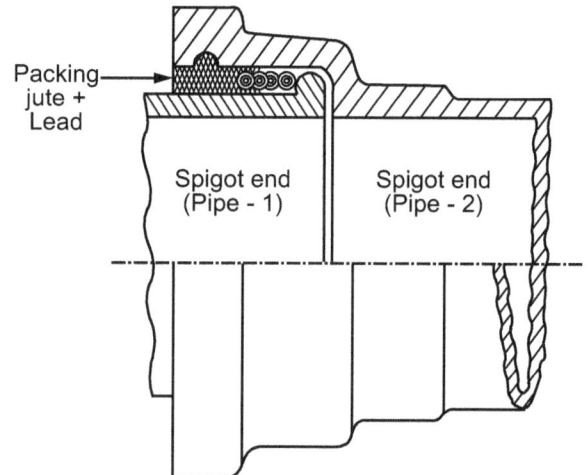

Fig. 3.13 : Socket and spigot joint

3.12 HYDRAULIC JOINT

It is used where fluids are to be transported under high pressure (50 to 80 kgf/cm^2). The flanges are very thick, integral with pipes and cast oval shaped. One of the flanges is provided with a circular spigot at the centre while the other is provided with a socket at the centre. The spigot enters the socket in other flange with a packing in between. The flanges are held tightly close together by two nuts and bolts (Refer Fig. 3.14). For very high pressures, steel pipes are used.

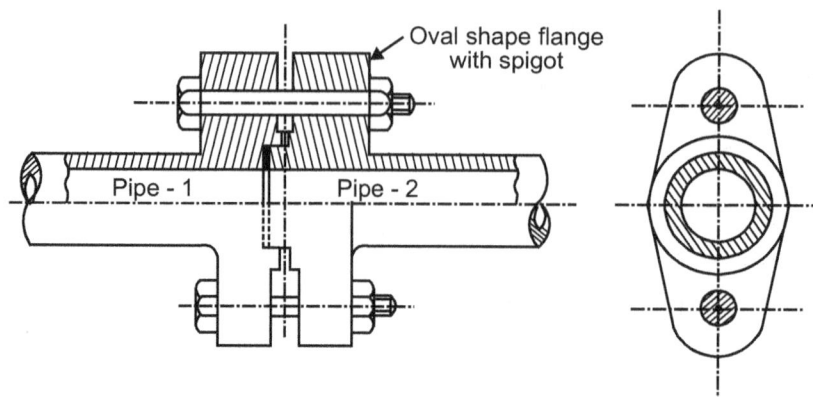

Fig. 3.14 : Hydraulic joint

3.13 EXPANSION JOINTS : LOOP AND CORRUGATED

In case of piping systems which carries steam at high pressures, a provision is usually made to permit longitudinal expansion or contraction of metal due to variations in temperature. Expansion joints in the form of a copper corrugated expansion bellows
[Fig. 3.15 (a)] or a loop made of copper pipe [Fig. 3.15 (b) and (c)] placed between the pipes at suitable intervals readily accommodate such alteration in length of the piping. The bellows piece is brazed to mild steel flanges.

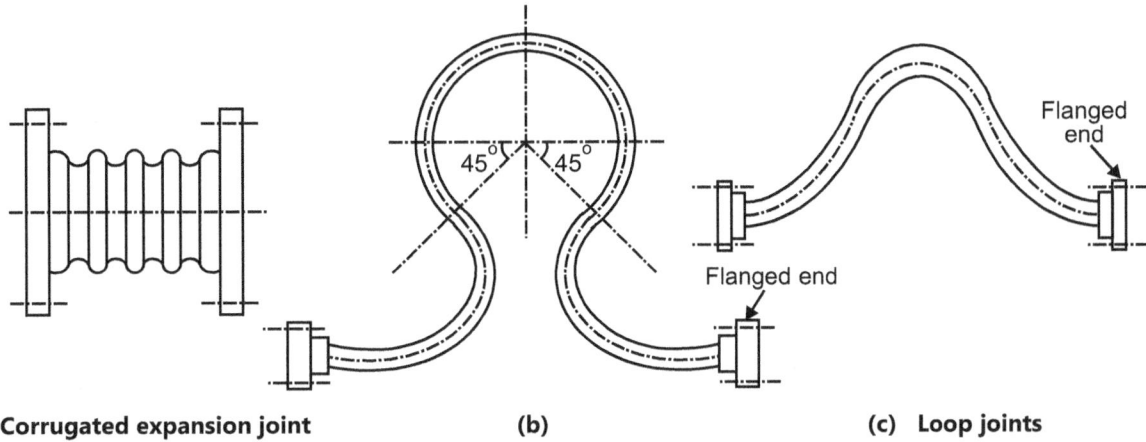

(a) Corrugated expansion joint   (b)   (c) Loop joints

Fig. 3.15 : Expansion joints

3.14 C. I. FLANGES

Cast iron is used for pipes of diameters - 50 mm to 1500 mm. These pipes are used for water, sewage, etc. Cast iron pipes of small diameter are connected by a flange joint.

Cast Iron Flange Joint :

A cast iron flange cast with the pipe is shown in Fig. 3.16. The flange faces are machined at right angles to the axis of the pipe to ensure a correct alignment of the pipes when joined together. The joint is achieved by connecting the flanges together by bolts and nuts. For preventing leakage through the joint, a packing of soft material such as rubber, canvas, etc. is interposed in between the flanges.

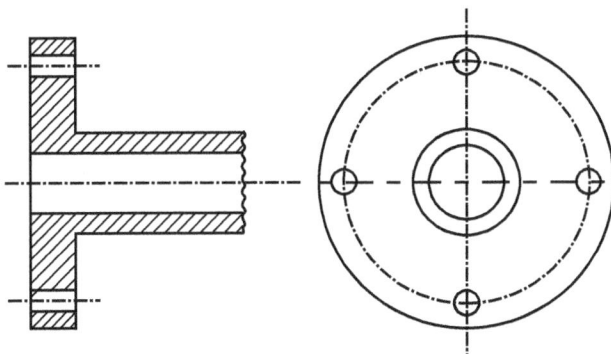

Fig. 3.16 : A flange cast with pipe

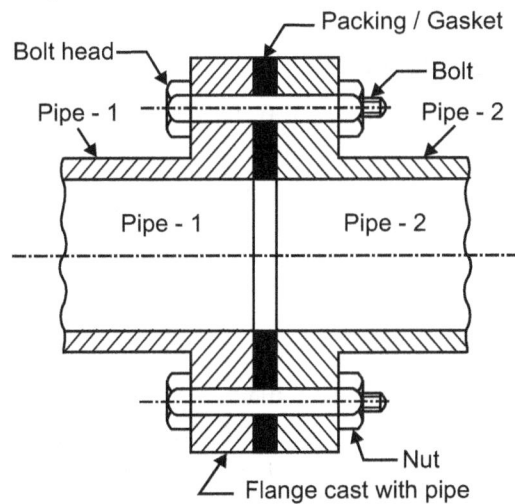

Fig. 3.17 : Cast-iron flanged joint

3.15 FLANGE FACINGS

Flanges are available with a variety of faces. The faces are machined to specific finish. Based upon the width of gasket covering the flange facing, we have : Wide-face flanges and Narrow-face flanges. In case of wide-face flanges, the gasket extends over the full width of the flange face and in case of narrow-face flanges, the gasket does not extend beyond the inside of the bolt holes.

In case of the flanges with raised faces, a certain portion of the flange face is raised over which the gasket is placed. They are used extensively for average service conditions. In case of the flanges with a ring facing, the ring facing is formed by making identical grooves (usually trapezoidal in shape) on both the flange facings. In this case, the gasket is in the form of a ring and it fits into the grooves. This type of the flange facing offers the greatest protection under severe service conditions and with use of hazardous fluids. It is used extensively in petroleum, petrochemical, and high pressure service. In case of male and female facings, one flange facing is having a groove and the other facing is having a raised ring (tongue). These confine the gaskets and used widely on heat exchangers.

(a) Plain face   **(b) Raised face**   **(c) Male and female**

(d) Ring facing   **(e) Tongue and groove facing**

Fig. 3.18 : Flange facings

3.16 FLANGE TYPES

Whenever we require the detachable type of joint between any two components, then they must be provided with flanges, with arrangement for bolting.

So heads, vessel shells, nozzles, and piping are provided with flanges. The bolted flanged connections that are easily removable facilitate disassembly of different components.

A flanged joint consists of a pair of flanges, one each attached to the components to be joined/connected. The flanges are held securely together by a series of bolts or studs. A gasket is interposed (placed) between the flange facings to have a leak-proof joint. As we go on tightening the nuts, the flanges come close to each other, gasket gets compressed and this causes yielding of the gasket surface thus sealing the irregular surface of the flange faces.

A great variety of types and sizes of flanges are available for various pressure services. Flanges are fabricated either by casting, forging or formed from plates.

3.16.1 Slip-on Flanges

It is used extensively because of its greater ease of alignment in welding assembly and because of its low cost. It is used for moderate services.

Fig. 3.19 : Slip-on flange

3.16.2 Welded-neck Flanges

These flanges are having a long, tapered hub between the flange ring and the weld joint. The hub of this flange increases its strength. Such flanges are used for extreme service conditions – wide fluctuations in temperature or pressure, high pressure, high temperature, and sub zero temperatures.

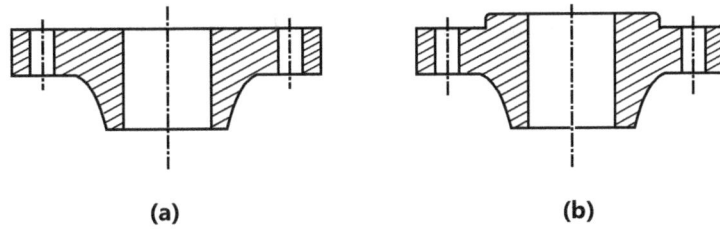

(a)   (b)

Fig. 3.20 : Welded-neck flanges

3.16.3 Hub Type Flanges

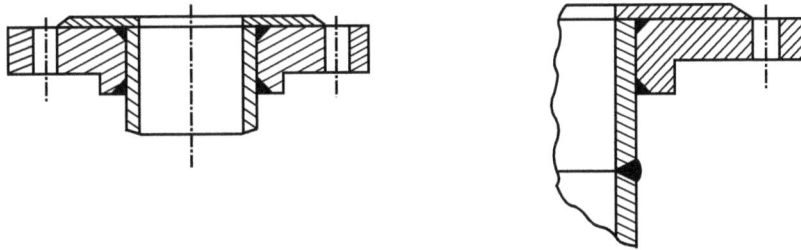

Fig. 3.21 : Hub type flange with stainless steel lining (for SS vessels)

3.16.4 Lap Type Flanges

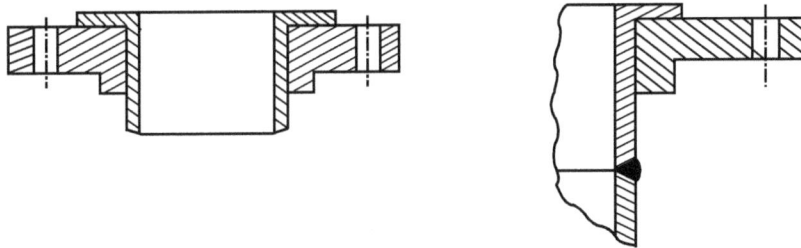

Fig. 3.22 : Lap joint flange (and lab joint stub)

Lap joint flanges are usually used with a lap joint stub. These flanges are used where frequent dismantling for cleaning or inspection is required or where it is required to rotate the pipe by swirling the flange. With these flanges, bolts, holes are easily aligned and this makes the erection of vessels of large diameters and stiff piping simple.

3.16.5 Screwed Flanges

These flanges are quickly connected to a threaded pipe without welding. Threaded connection is susceptible to leakage under any type of cyclic operation.

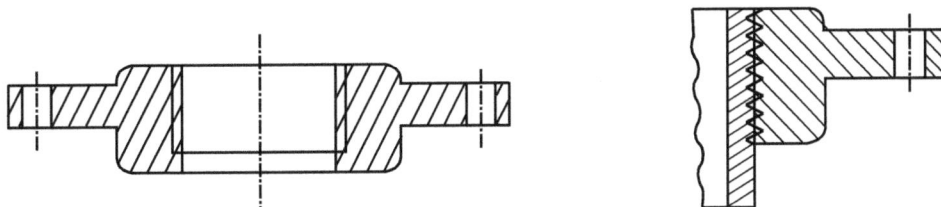

Fig. 3.23 : Screwed flange

Fig. 3.24 : Ring flange for non-pressure service

SUPPORTS FOR PIPES AND VESSELS

4.1 HANGER SUPPORTS

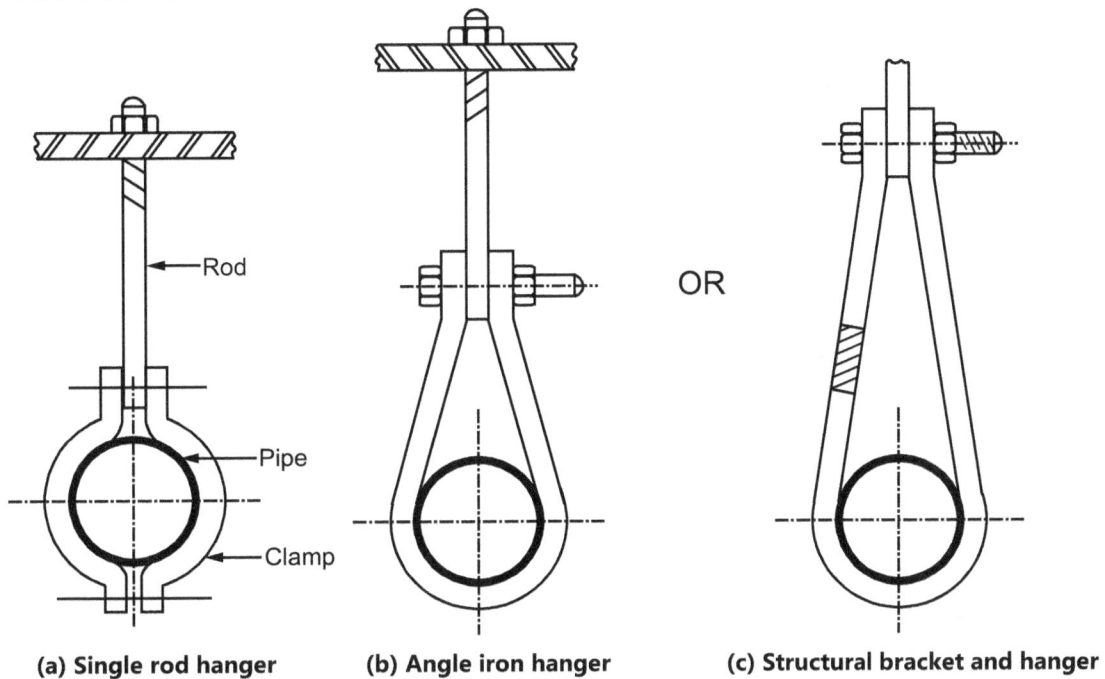

(a) Single rod hanger   **(b) Angle iron hanger**   **(c) Structural bracket and hanger**

Hangers are used as typical indoor supports for piping under flooring and platforms [Fig. 4.1 (b)]. These require taller support structures. Hanger rods may be pipe straps, chains, bars, or threaded rods that permit free movement for thermal expansion or contraction.

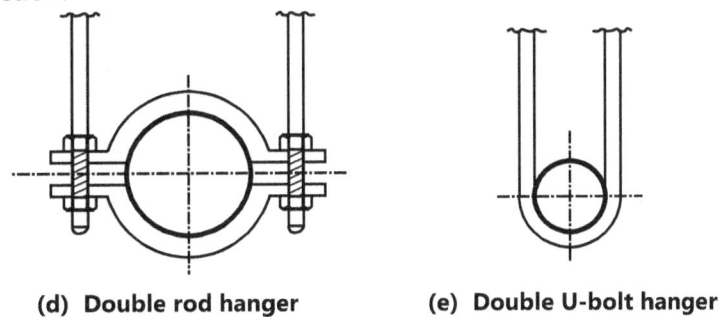

(d) Double rod hanger   **(e) Double U-bolt hanger**

Fig. 4.1 : Hanger supports

4.2 ROLLER SUPPORT

Steam pipes are not clamped rigidly but are suspended on hangers or free supported on rollers to allow for alteration in length (to permit free movement for thermal expansion or contraction).

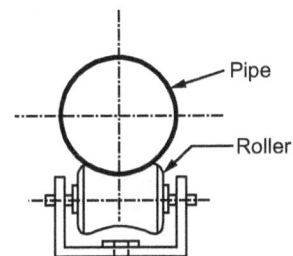

Fig. 4.2 : Roller support

(4.1)

4.3 YARD PIPING SUPPORT

A typical outdoor support for multiple group piping uses horizontal steel beams supported by structural steel stanchions (stanchion - an upright bar, post or frame forming a support).

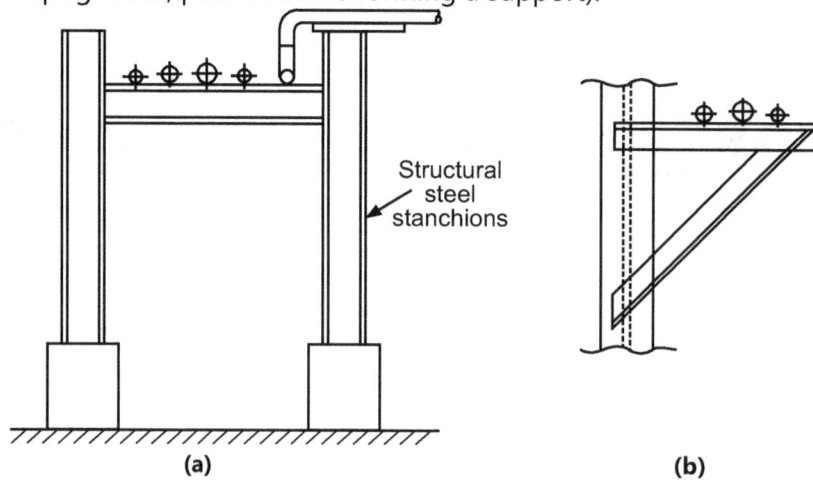

Fig. 4.3 : (a) Typical outdoor overhead pipe rack, (b) Small bank of lines on bracket

4.4 SUPPORTS FOR VESSELS

Various methods are used/adopted for supporting cylindrical vessels. Vertical vessels are supported by brackets (or lugs), legs, or skirt while horizontal vessels are normally supported by saddles. The selection of a suitable type of support depends upon the size (dimensions) of the vessel, floor space available, wall thickness of the vessel, elevation of the vessel in relation to the ground or floor, the materials of construction and the operating temperature.

4.4.1 Vertical Vessels

Bracket or Lug Supports

Supports of this type can be easily fabricated from plates and attached to the vessel wall with minimum welding length and are made to rest on short columns or on beams of a structure depending upon the elevation needed. Bracket supports are most suitable for vessels with thick walls. In case of thin walled vessels, the area where a bracket is to be attached is reinforced by use of a pad. The pad is welded to the shell and the bracket is then welded to the pad [Fig. 4.4]. The minimum number of supports required are two (for small vessels). Depending upon the size of a vessel, number of brackets are to be used and are to be placed at an equal angle along the periphery of the vessel. Vessels that are not tool tall, e.g., batch reactor, crystallisers, dilution tanks etc. are supported by bracket supports.

The bracket supports are inexpensive, easily attached to the vessels, and are easily leveled. The vessels that are not tool tall, e.g., batch reactor, crystalliser, dilution tanks, etc. are supported by bracket supports.

The bracket support shown in Fig. 4.4 consists of two vertical gusset plates with two horizontal plate stiffeners that are welded to the shell by fillet welds.

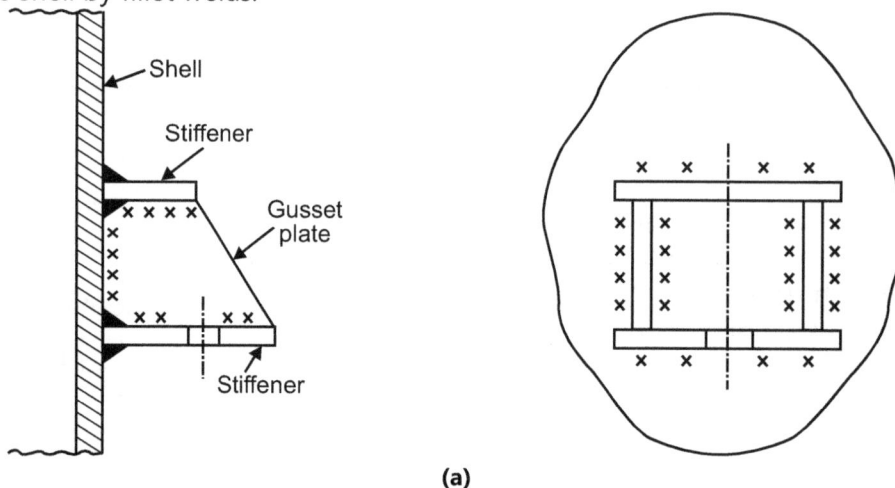

(a)

(b)

(c)

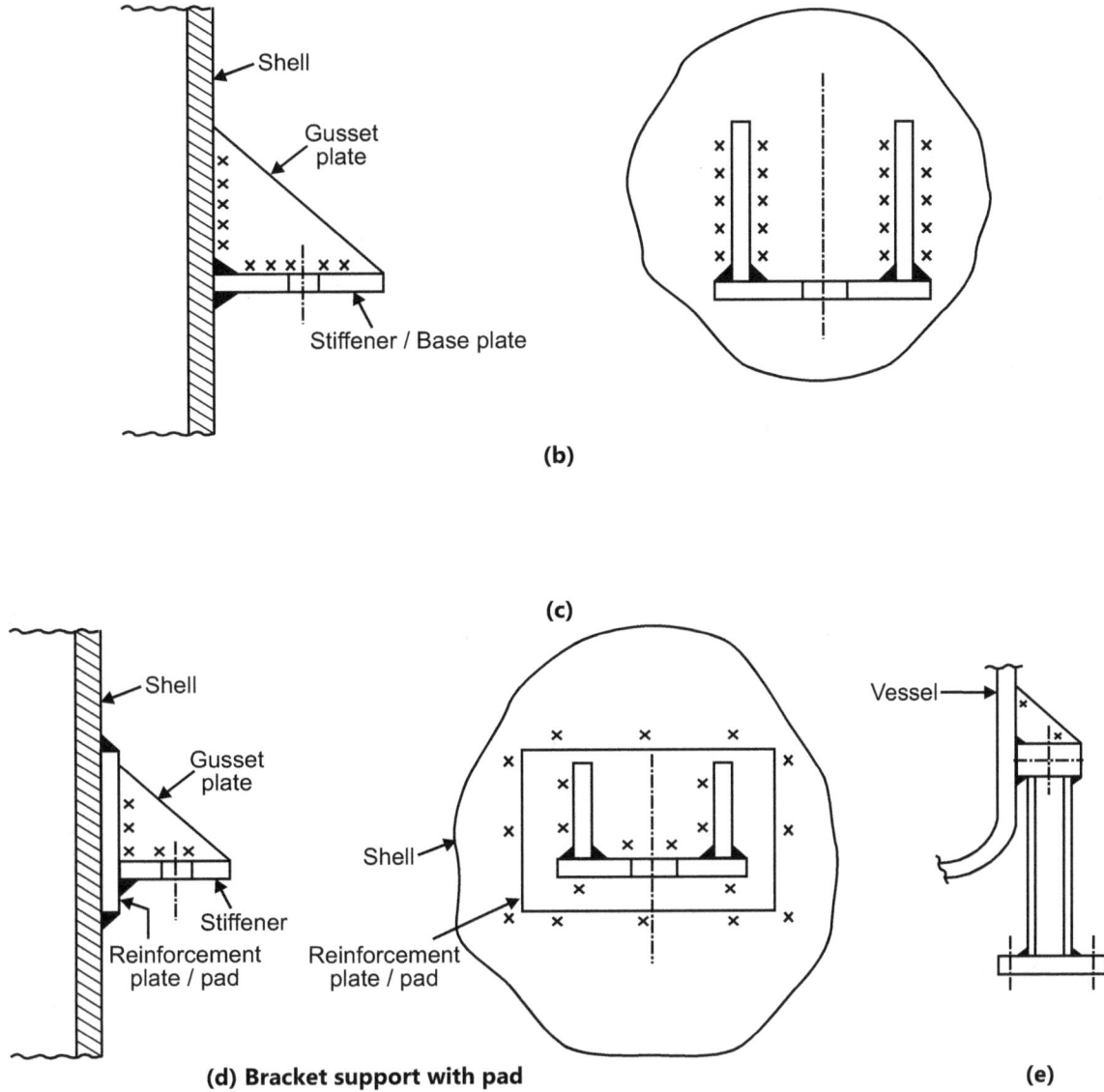

(d) Bracket support with pad   **(e)**

Fig. 4.4 : Bracket supports

Leg Supports

Structural sections such as angles, channels can be directly welded to the pressure vessel shell in order to form vertical legs (supports) as shown in Fig. 4.5. This type of support is used only for small vessels.

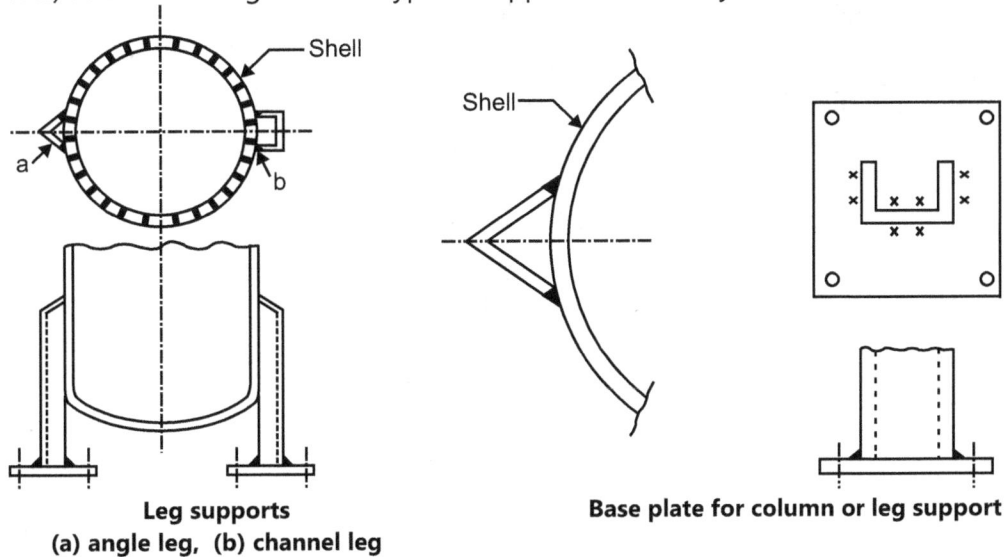

Leg supports
(a) angle leg, (b) channel leg   **Base plate for column or leg support**

Fig. 4.5 : Leg supports

Skirt Supports

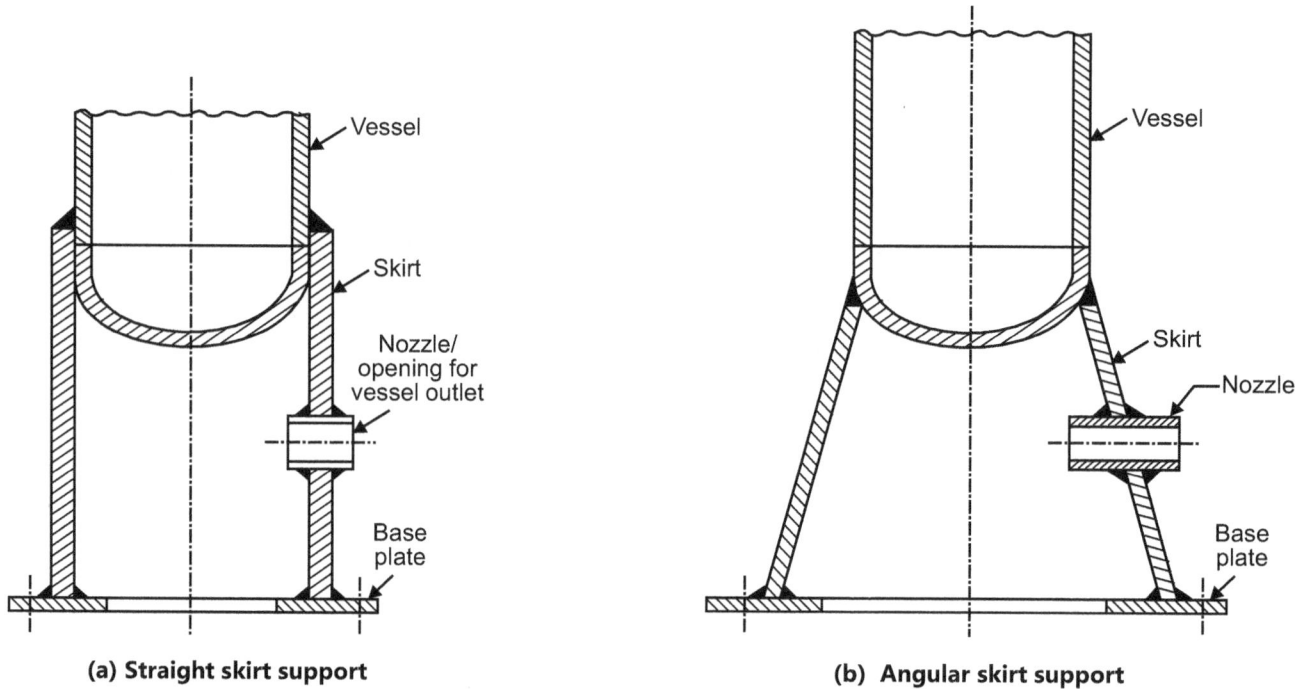

(a) Straight skirt support

(b) Angular skirt support

Fig. 4.6 : Skirt supports

Tall vertical vessels are usually supported by cylindrical steel shells called skirts.

A cylindrical skirt is an economical design for a support for a tall vertical vessel. The skirt may be welded directly to the bottom dished head, flush with the shell, or to the outside of the shell. A bearing plate is welded to the bottom of the skirt. The bearing plate rests on a concrete foundation and is securely anchored to the foundation by means of anchor bolts fixed firmly in concrete in order to prevent overturning from the bending moments induced by wind or seismic loads. The bearing plate may be a single flat ring with or without gussets. Alternately a bolting chair is used for securing the skirt to the foundation. The bolting chair is formed by two flat rings - a bearing plate and a compression plate with gusset plates in between. [Fig. 4.8].

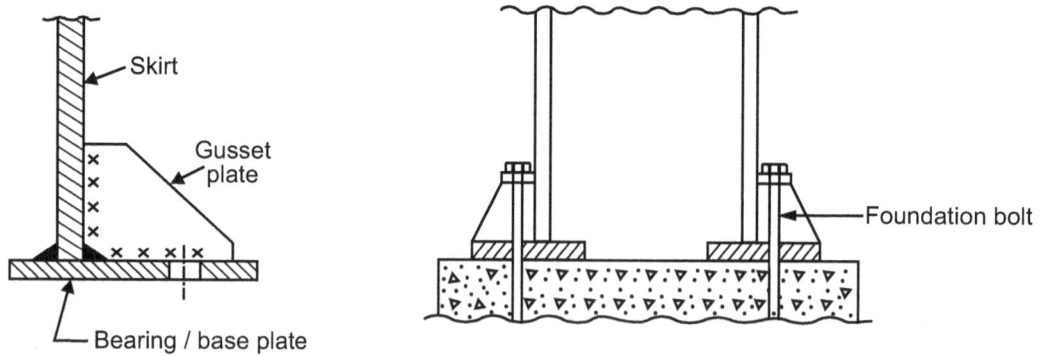

Fig. 4.7 : Ring bearing plate with a gusset plate

If the required bearing plate thickness is more than 18 mm, it is advisable to use a number of bolting chairs along the periphery of the skirt. For large diameter vessels, external bolting chair is suitable.

Fig. 4.8 : External bolting chair

4.4.2 Horizontal Vessel

Saddle Supports

Horizontal cylindrical pressure vessels are commonly supported by saddle supports. They are placed at two positions. For vessels in which supports at more than two positions are unavoidable, supports in the form of rings are preferable. For thin walled vessels or vessels under vacuum, it is necessary to provide ring supports. In case of small vessels, simple leg supports may be used. [Fig. 4.9].

By attaching a wear plate to the shell directly over the saddle (somewhat larger than the surface of the saddle), the stresses in the shell band adjoining the saddle are reduced. Whenever necessary the vessel shell is strengthened ring stiffeners, located on the shell area surrounding the saddle. These are in the form of a ring welded either inside or outside the shell. [Fig. 4.11].

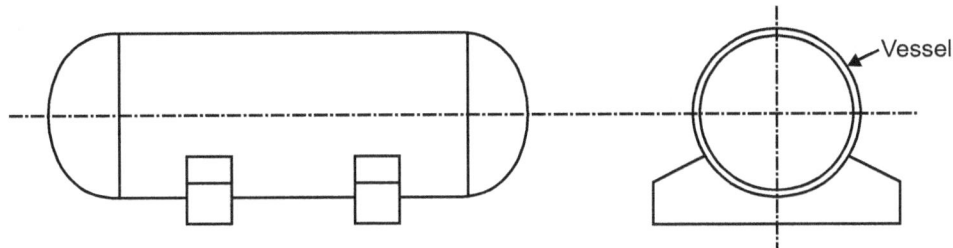

(a) Saddle support (Plate type)

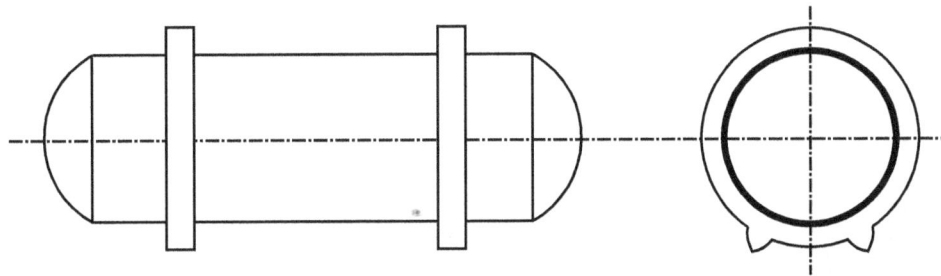

(b) Saddle support (Ring type)

Fig. 4.9

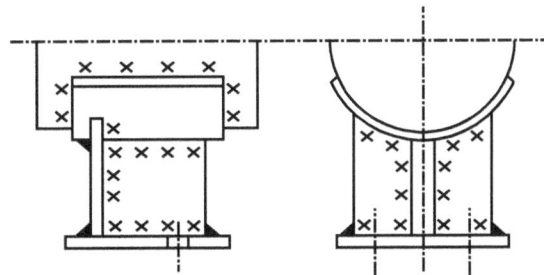

Fig. 4.10 : Wear plate for saddle

(a) Internal stiffening ring   **(b) External stiffening ring**

Fig. 4.11

● ● ●

FABRICATION DRAWING

This chapter covers the fabrication drawing of process equipments such as heat exchanger, batch reactor, etc. Once the design of a process equipment is done, a fabrication drawing of the process equipment is prepared prior to the fabrication of the equipment. The fabrication drawing comprises of assembly and detailed drawings, specifying all requirements and show how the component pieces are connected to each other by welding and bolting.

5.1 HEAT EXCHANGERS

A heat exchanger is a process equipment used for transferring heat from one fluid to another fluid through a separating wall. Usually, heat exchangers are classified according to the functions for which they are employed. Shell and tube heat exchangers are widely used in industry. The shell and tube heat exchanger consists of a number of parallel tubes enclosed in a cylindrical shell. One of the fluids flows through the shell and other flows through the tubes. One which flows through the shell is called the shell side fluid and that flowing through the tubes is called the tube side fluid. When none of the fluids condenses or evaporates, the unit is called as a heat exchanger. In this case, only sensible heat transfer takes place from one process fluid to another. When one of the fluids, either in the tube or the shell condenses, the unit is known as a condenser or as a heater, based on whether the primary/basic purpose of the unit is to condense one fluid or to heat the other. In this case, latent heat transfer takes place. Likewise, when one of the fluids evaporates, the unit is called as an evaporator or as a cooler, based on whether the primary purpose is to evaporate one fluid or to cool the other.

Shell and tube heat exchangers, e.g., plate type heat exchanger, etc. are used in special cases where the standard forms of tubular exchangers are not suitable. Here only shell and tube heat exchangers are considered.

Shell and tube heat exchangers are built of a shell in which a number of tubes are mounted by means of tube sheets. Many versions of the basic type are available, the difference lies mainly in the detailed features of construction. According to the mechanical configuration, shell and tube heat exchangers are classified as :

(i)　　Fixed tube sheet,　(ii)　Internal floating head

(iii)　　Outside packed floating head

(iv)　　Reboiler (with internal floating head or U-tube type)

The main components of the above cited heat exchangers are : (1) shell, (2) shell cover, (3) tubes, (4) tube sheet, (5) tie rods and spacers, (6) baffles, (7) channel, (8) channel cover, (9) pass portions, (10) nozzles, (11) flanges and (12) supports.

Fixed tube sheet heat exchanger : (Refer Fig. 5.1)

In case of these heat exchangers, the shell is welded to two tube sheets, one each at either end. The tube sheets also serve as flanges for the attachment of the channels or bonnets. In this exchanger, it is necessary to provide expansion bellows on the shell to eliminate excessive stresses in the shell and tubes due to differential thermal expansion. It is used only where the shell side fluid is clean as mechanical cleaning, and usual inspection of the outside of tubes is not possible with a non-removable tube-bundle.

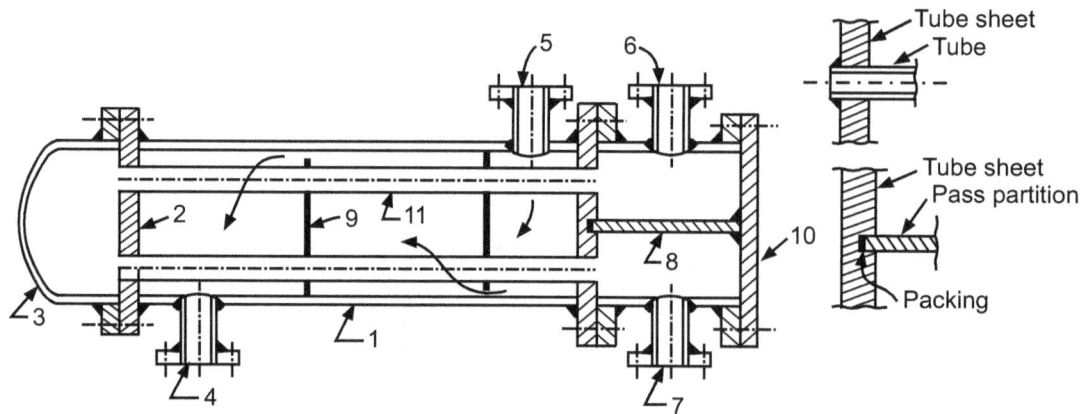

1 - shell, 2 - tube sheet, 3 - cover, 4, 5 - shell side nozzle inlet/outlet, 6, 7 - tube nozzle-inlet/outlet, 8 - pass partition, 9 - baffle, 10 - channel cover, 11 - tube, Section lines are not shown for shell, cover and nozzles

Fig. 5.1 : Fixed tube-sheet shell and tube heat exchanger (1-2 pass)

U-Tube Heat Exchanger

In this type of heat exchanger, the tube bundle consists of U-shaped tubes, both ends of which are fixed to a single stationary tube sheet. This exchanger requires only one tube sheet. The tube bundle can be removed for cleaning of the tubes from outside. The inside of tubes can be cleaned only by chemical means. These exchangers are usually employed for high pressure and temperature applications where a single tube sheet results in considerable reduction in cost. (Fig. 5.2).

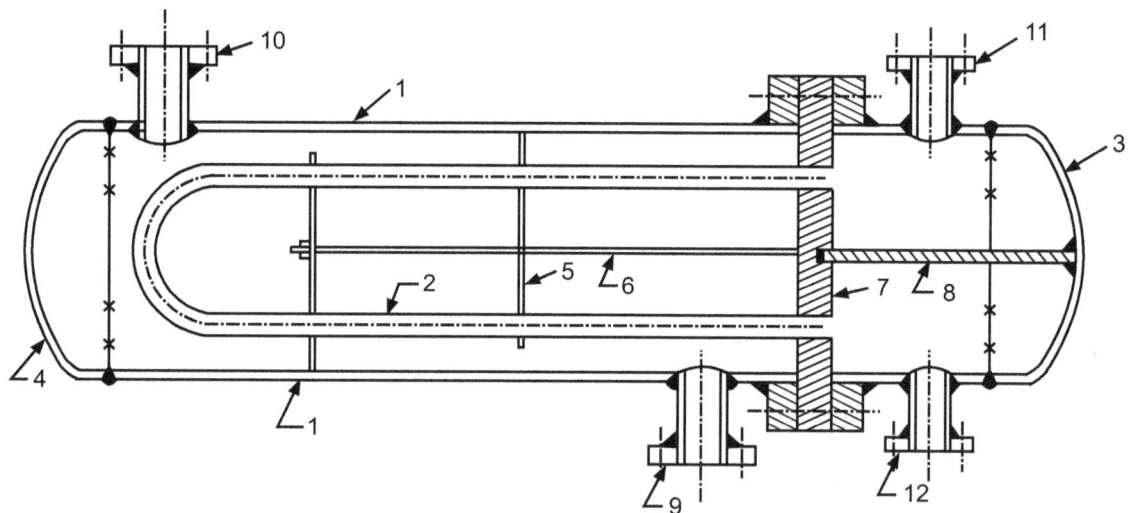

1 - shell, 2 - U-tube, 3 - channel cover, 4 - cover, 5 - baffle, 6 - tie rod, 7 - tube sheet,

8 - pass partition, 9, 10 - shell inlet-outlet nozzle, 11, 12 - tube side inlet-outlet nozzle

Section lines are not shown for shell, nozzles, covers, etc.

Fig. 5.2 : U-tube heat exchanger

Reboiler Exchanger

It is either provided with an internal floating head arrangement or a U-tube arrangement. The shell of this exchanger is of a larger diameter to provide a vapour space above the tube-bundle. This exchanger (kettle type reboiler) is located at the bottom of a distillation column for converting the liquid at the bottom of the column into vapour. (Fig. 5.3).

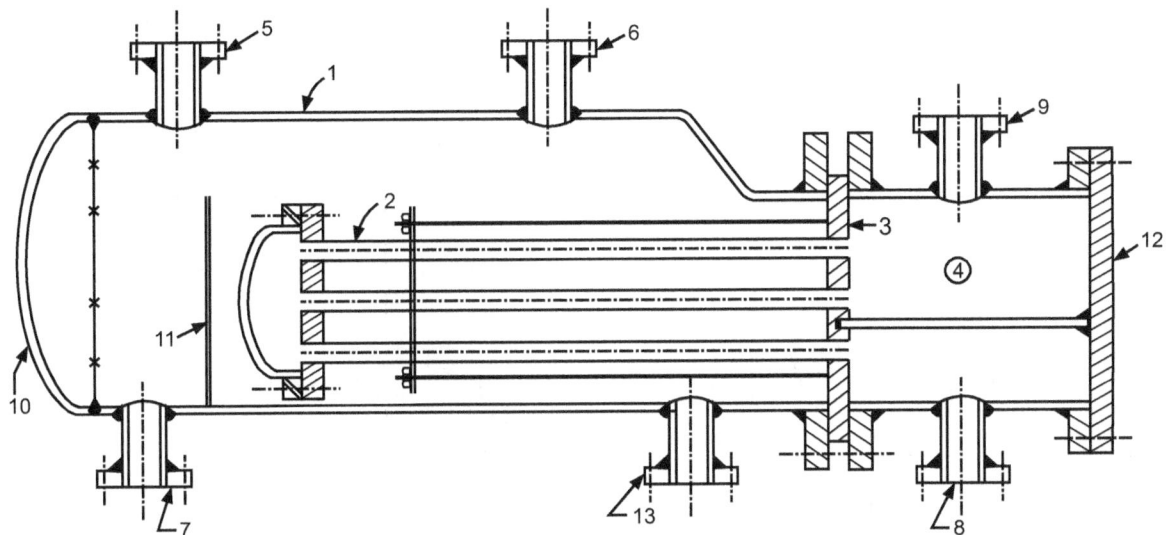

1 - shell, 2 - tube bundle, 3 - tube sheet, 4 - channel, 5, 6 - vapour outlet, 7 liquid outlet,

8, 9 - tube side nozzle, 10 - shell cover, 11 - weir, 12 - channel cover, 13 - liquid inlet

Fig. 5.3 : Kettle reboiler

Shell : It is usually a cylindrical casing through which one of the fluid flows in one or more passes. It may be cut to the required length from a standard pipe upto 600 mm diameter or fabricated from plates. The minimum thickness of the shell made out of carbon steel varies from 5 mm to 11 mm depending upon the diameter. The ratio of the length of tube to the diameter of shell for liquid-liquid exchangers varies from 4 : 1 to 8 : 1.

Tubes : Standard heat exchanger tubes which are used in many industrial processes may be of various sizes and lengths. The outside diameter of tubes varies from 6 to 40 mm. The tubes with outside diameters of 19 mm and 25 mm are very common. The tube lengths used are 0.5, 2.5, 3, 4, 5 and 6 meters. The wall thickness of the tubes is usually expressed in terms of Birmingham Wire Gauge (BWG). The thickness depends upon the material of construction and diameter. For 19 or 25 mm outside diameter, a tube of mild steel with 10 or 12 BWG is common. The tubes are laid out either on a square pitch or on an equilateral triangular pitch. The advantage of square pitch is that it permits external cleaning of the tubes and causes a low pressure drop on the shell side fluid. If the fluid is very clean, a triangular pitch is used. A triangular pitch arrangement incorporates a larger number of tubes in a given shell diameter than with a square pitch arrangement and usually creates a large turbulence in the shell side fluid.

Tube Sheet

A tube sheet is a flat plate with a provision for making a gasketed joint, around the periphery. In the tube sheet, a large number of holes are drilled according to the pitch requirements of the tubes. The tubes are laid out either on an equilateral triangular pitch or a square pitch. The minimum pitch is 1.25 times the outside diameter of tubes (Fig. 5.4).

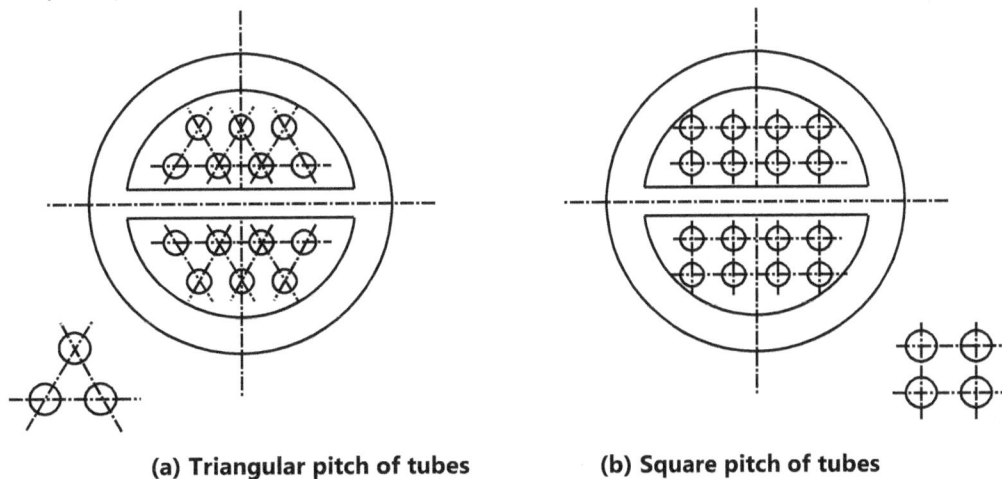

(a) Triangular pitch of tubes   **(b) Square pitch of tubes**

Fig. 5.4 : Tube sheet

Methods of fixing tubes to tube sheet :

The common method of fixing the tubes in a tube sheet consisting of expanding the ends of the tubes located in the tube sheet holes by means of a rotating, roller expanding tool. The holes in the tube sheet are drilled undersize and are then reamed to a diameter slightly larger than the outside diameter of the tube. When the tubes have a small diameter, then tubes are soldered or brazed into the tube sheet holes. The tubes can also be welded in the tube sheet holes but this method makes the tube replacement very difficult. Fig. 5.5 shows various methods of fixing the tubes in the tube sheet.

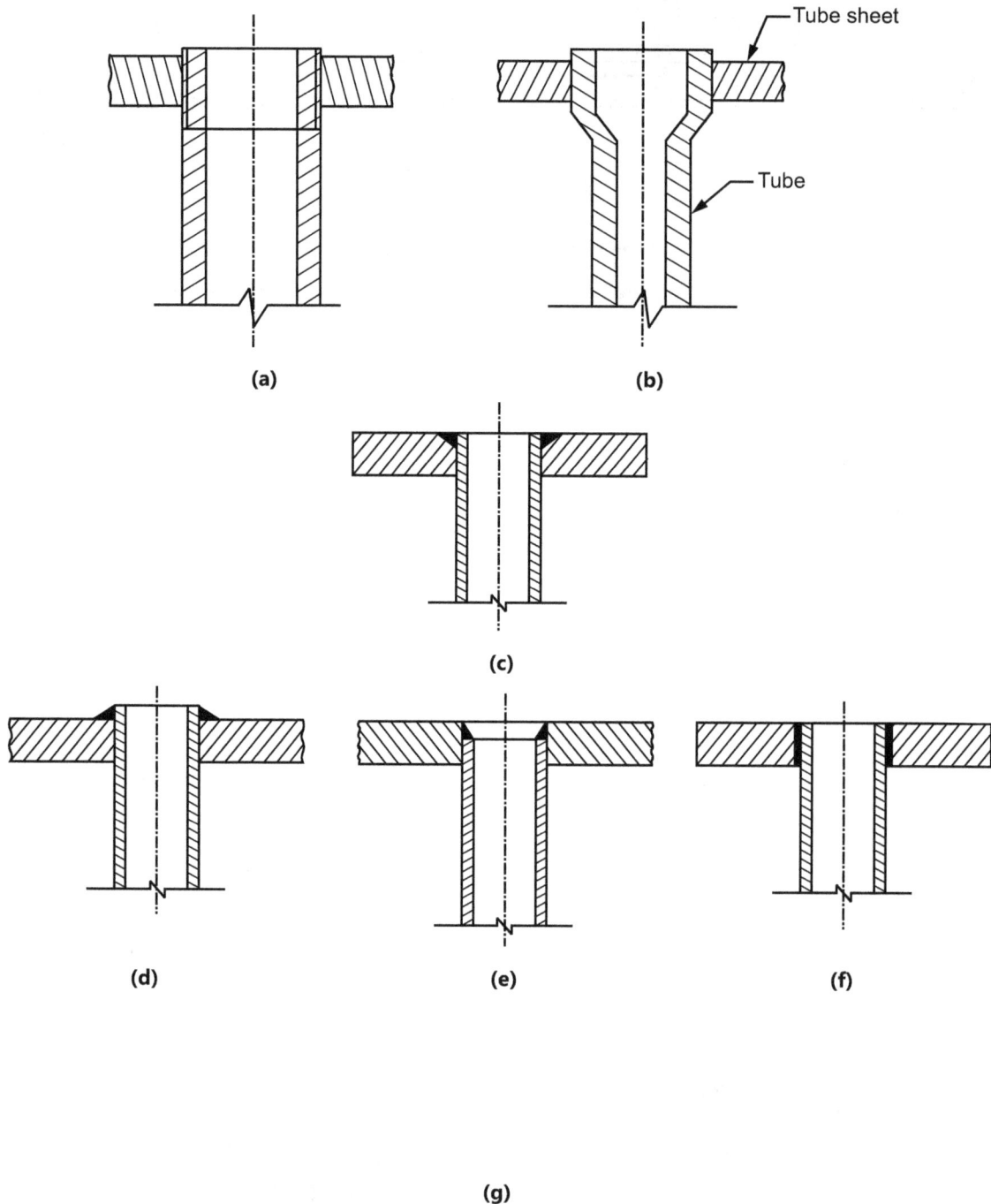

(a) screwed tube, (b) and (c) rolled tubes, (d), (e) and (f) welded tubes, (g) brazed tube

Fig. 5.5 : Methods of fixing tubes to tube sheet

Shell side and Tube side passes :

The direction of flow of the shell side and tube side fluids can be changed by use of different flow paths known as passes. The passes are provided to obtain higher velocities and to provide longer paths for the fluid to travel without increasing the length of the exchanger. The shell side passes are single pass, two pass, single split pass and double split pass, whereas the tube side passes are one, two, four, six, etc. (Figs. 5.6 and 5.7).

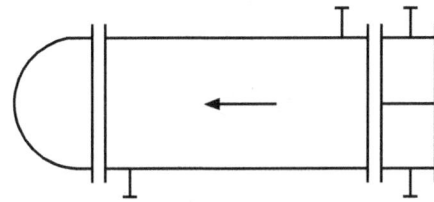

Fig. 5.6 : (a) Single pass

The passes on the shell side are formed by use of baffles provided in the shell while those on the tube side are formed by partitions provided in the channels and shell cover.

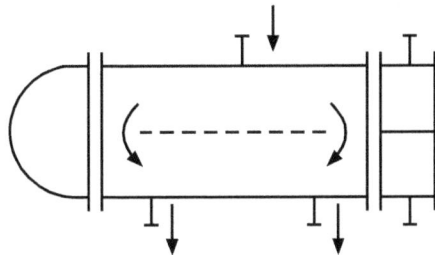

(b) Single split pass   **(c) Two passes**

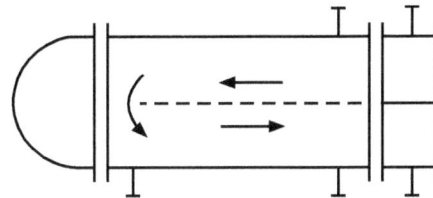

Fig. 5.6 : Shell side passes

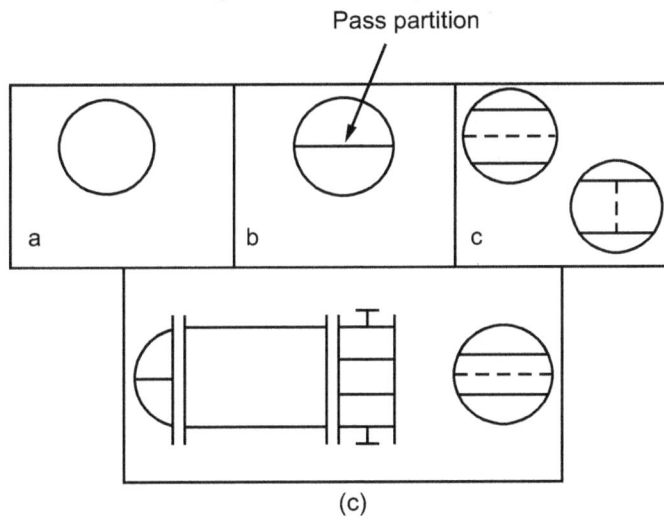

Pass partition

(a) Single pass, (b) Two passes and (c) Four passes

Fig. 5.7 : Tube side passes

Tube Sheet, Channel and Shell Joints

To hold the tube sheet between shell and channel, also for channel covers, flanged joints are used. The flanges used may be ring type or welding neck type. Flange facings may be raise face, male and female or tongue and groove (Fig. 5.8).

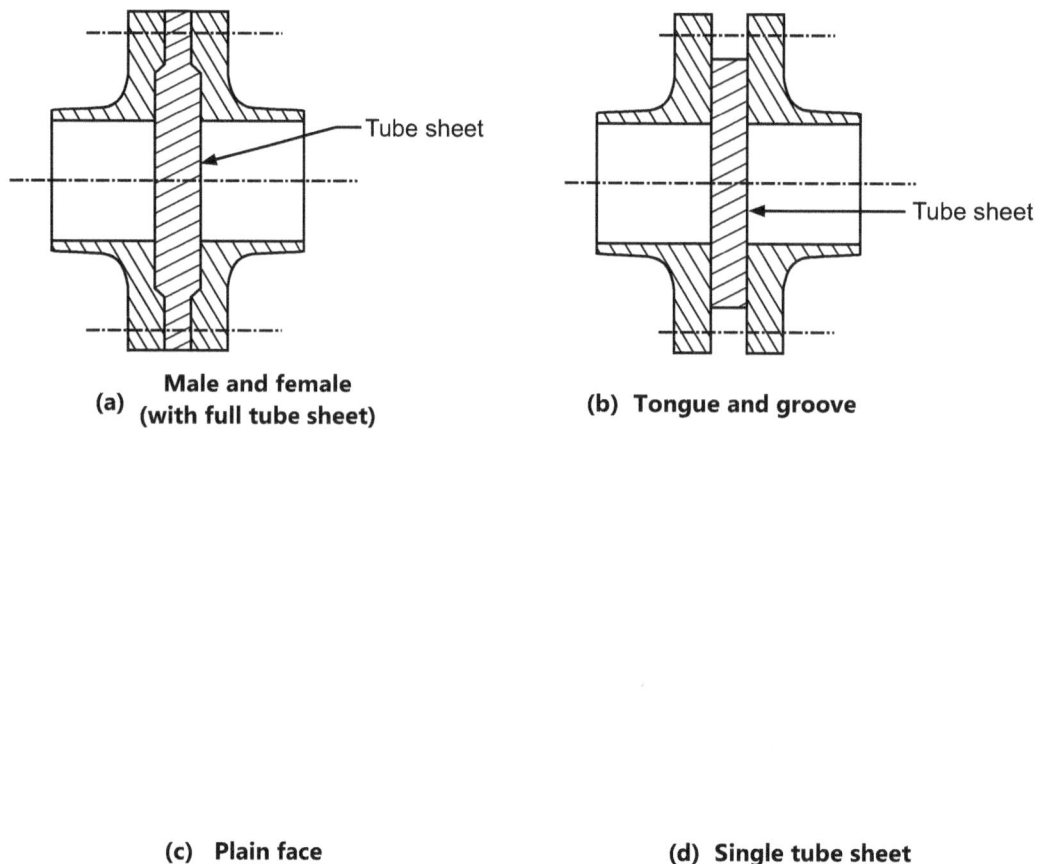

(a) **Male and female (with full tube sheet)**   **(b)** **Tongue and groove**

(c) **Plain face**   **(d)** **Single tube sheet**

Fig. 5.8 : Flanged joint with tube sheet

Expansion Bellow or Diaphragm

In case of fixed tube-sheet heat exchangers, it is necessary to make a provision to allow for differences in the expansion of the shell and tube because of rise in temperature which otherwise induce considerable stresses in the tubes and shell. In order to reduce the thermal stresses, a fairly flexible element is interpositioned in the comparatively stiff shell of the exchanger. The flexible element is known as the expansion bellow or diaphragm. It has sufficient flexibility and it permits constrained expansion or contraction of the shell. Fig. 5.9 shows an expansion diaphragm consisting of two dish shaped discs each welded to the shell. The discs are welded together to form a diaphragm.

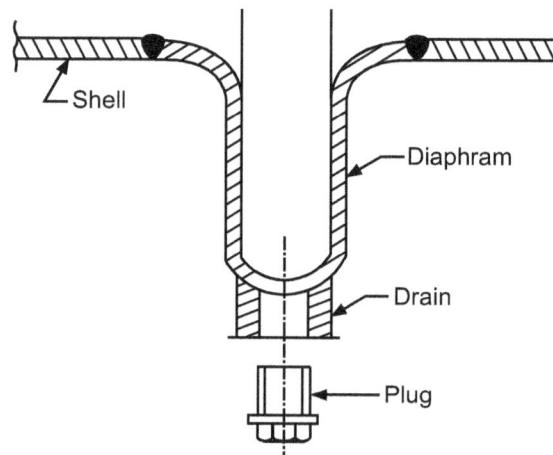

Fig. 5.9 : Expansion diaphragm

Baffles and tie rods :

Baffles are commonly employed within the shell to increase the rate of heat transfer by increasing the velocity and turbulence of the shell side fluid and also as structural supports for tubes and dampers against vibration. The baffles cause the fluid to flow through the shell at right angles to the axes of the tubes. To avoid bypassing of the shell side fluid, the clearance between the baffles and shell, and baffles and tubes must be minimum.

The centre-to-centre distance between adjacent baffles is known as the baffle spacing or baffle pitch. The baffle spacing should not be greater than the inside diameter of the shell and should not be less than one-fifth of the inside diameter of the shell. The optimum baffle spacing is 0.3 to 0.50 times the shell diameter.

The various transverse baffles used are segmental, disc and ring, orifice, etc. The **segmental baffle** is a drilled circular disk of sheet metal with one side cut away. **When the height of the baffle is 75% of the inside diameter of the shell, it is called 25% cut segmental baffle**. The 25% cut segmental baffle is the optimum one giving good heat transfer rates without excessive pressure drop. The segmental baffles are most commonly used. The baffle thickness usually ranges from 3 mm to 6 mm. Fig. 5.10 (a) shows a segmental baffle.

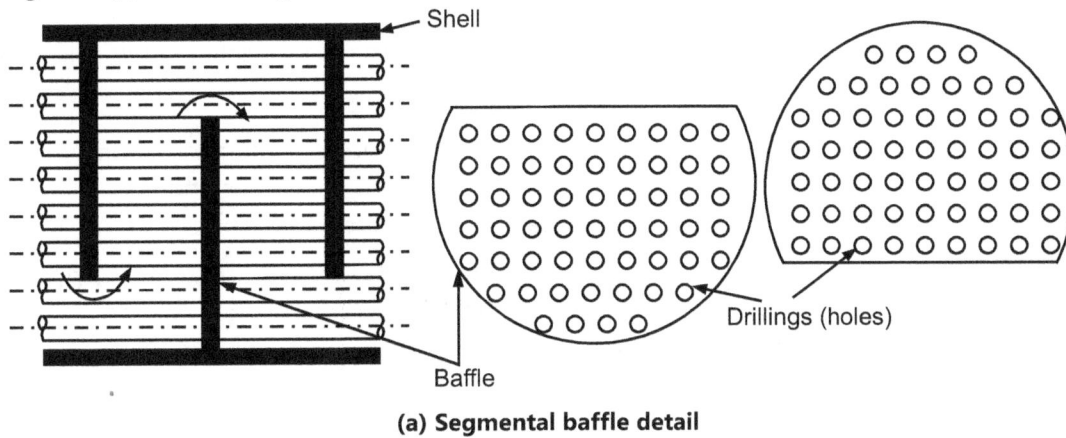

(a) Segmental baffle detail

(b) Disc and ring type baffle

Fig. 5.10

Tie rods are used to hold the baffles in place, with spacers to position/locate the baffles. Tie rods are fixed at one end in the tube sheet by making blind holes. Usually 4 to 6 tie rods with atleast 10 mm diameter are necessary.

5.2 BATCH REACTOR

The agitated reactors used in the industry to carry out chemical reactions may be classified according to their mode of operation. They may be operated batch-wise, semi-batch wise or continuously and thus, we have batch reactors, semibatch reactors and continuous stirred tank reactors (CSTRs).

A batch reactor/semi-batch reactor/CSTR consists of a vertical vessel equipped with a suitable agitator and either an external jacket or internal coils, or both for heating or cooling.

In case of batch reactors, the reactants are added to the empty reaction vessel, left to react for a certain time period under agitation and the contents are removed at once after completion of the reaction.

In case of semi-batch reactors, one of the reactants is charged initially to the reactor, while the other reactant is fed continuously into the reactor over a specified time period under agitation, holding of the reaction mass at a reaction temperature is done for a certain time period and the contents are removed after completion of the reaction.

In case of constant stirred tank reactors, the reactants flow continuously into the reactor and the products flow out continuously from the reactor. This reactor operates under steady-state conditions while the former two reactors operate under unsteady-state conditions.

These three reactors have the same construction features and in general they possess the following components :

(i) shell, (ii) head/cover/closure, (iii) nozzles, (iv) flange joints, (v) agitator, (vi) stuffing, (vii) baffles, (viii) cooling coil and/or heating jacket and (ix) support.

Supports for vessels are covered in Chapter 4 (4.4), flanges are covered in Chapter 3 and this chapter covers heads/covers at the end.

In a CSTR, some accumulation of the reaction mass is maintained in it so that the product flows out from a discharge connection provided near the top.

5.2.1 Shell

It is a cylindrical piece of required diameter, length and thickness. It is usually fabricated out of sheets or plates.

5.2.2 Nozzles

Nozzles or openings are provided either on the shell or head of a process equipment or on both as per functional requirements. These may serve as inlet/outlet connections, manholes, vents, handholes and drains. The nozzles used are circular or elliptical in shape and are generally provided with flanges (for further connections).

Nozzles are classified as integral, fabricated and formed. Integral nozzles are fabricated from a portion of the shell or head. The countour of nozzle is obtained by cutting and shaping the material of that portion. Fabricated nozzles are nothing but short pieces of pipes, tubes and plates. They are welded at an opening made in the shell or head. The formed nozzles with flanges are made to a specific size and shape by rolling or forging.

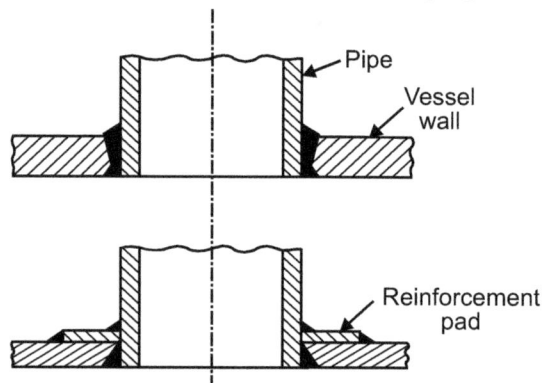

Fig. 5.11 : Attachment of pipes to vessel wall

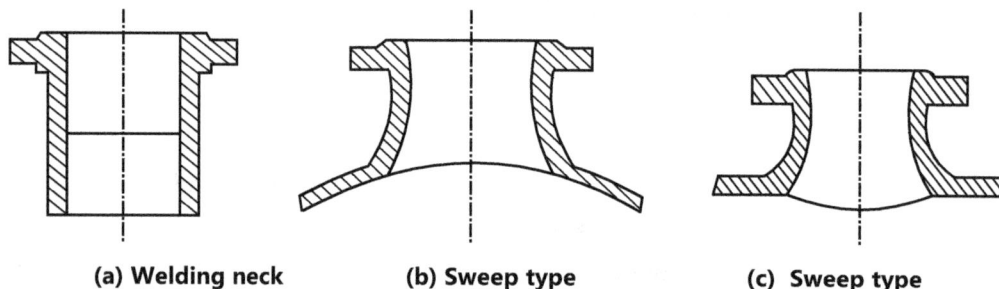

(a) Welding neck   (b) Sweep type   (c) Sweep type

Fig. 5.12 : Formed nozzles

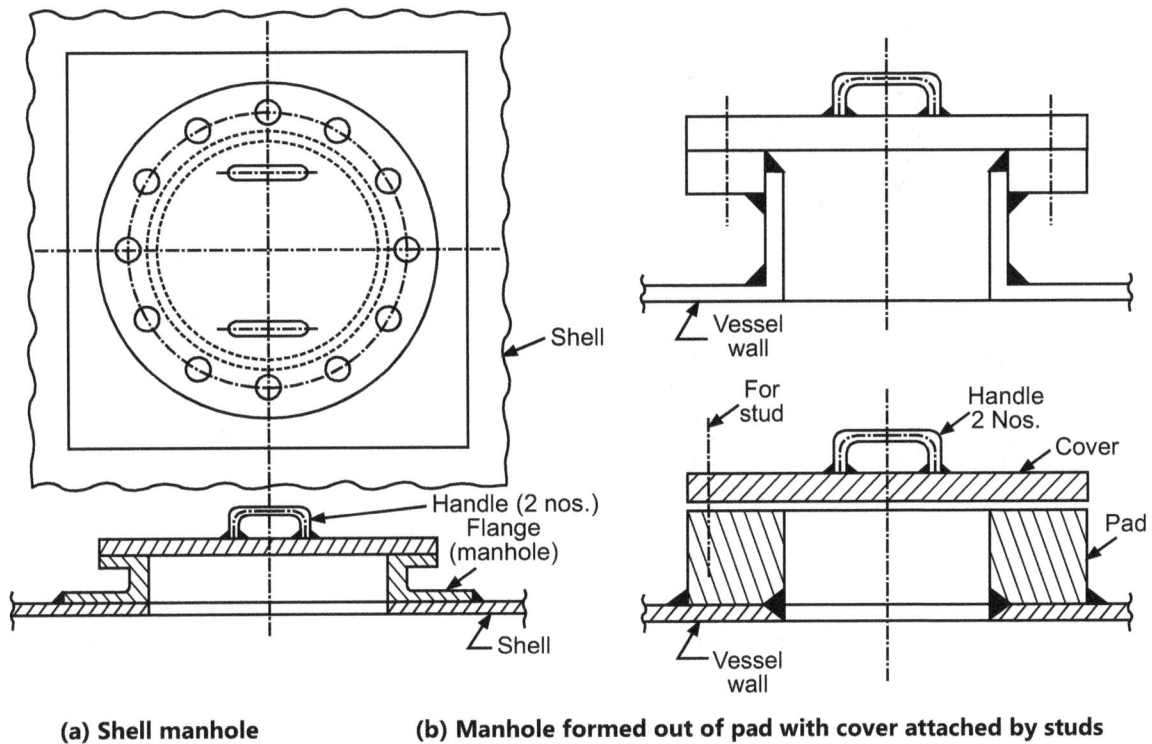

(a) Shell manhole   **(b) Manhole formed out of pad with cover attached by studs**

Fig. 5.13

5.2.3 Flanged Joints

For heads of pressure vessels to be of the detachable type, they must be provided with flanges. Such joints facilitate disassembly of different components very easily. A flanged joint consists of a pair of flanges, one each attached to the two components to be joined.

A gasket is interposed between the two flange faces to have a leak proof joint. The flanges are clamped together by a series of bolts or studs. As we go on tightening the nut or stud, the gasket gets compressed between the flange faces that results in yielding of its surface, hence sealing the irregular surface of the flange faces. Also refer to Fig. 5.14.

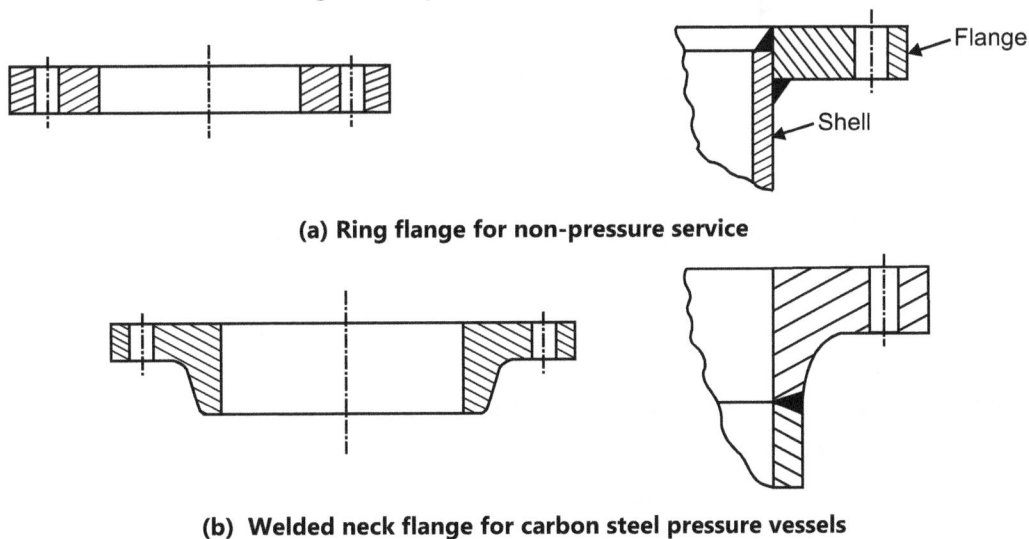

(a) Ring flange for non-pressure service

(b) Welded neck flange for carbon steel pressure vessels

Fig. 5.14 : Standard flanges and their attachment to shell

5.2.4 Jackets and Coils

Chemical reactions are accompanied by the evolution or absorption of heat. Therefore, chemical reactors are provided with the suitable means for supplying or removing the heat of reaction. For this purpose, indirect heat transfer systems are used. In such systems, the heat transfer fluid is supplied either in a jacket or in a coil. The jacket surrounds the vessel wall (reactor wall) and coil is incorporated within the vessel. Generally, a jacket is used for heating (to provide heat) and a coil is used for cooling (or remove heat) purpose. In most cases, heat is supplied by condensation of a vapour and for this jackets are used as they provide more space for condensation than in a coil. The turbulence is more in a coil than in a jacket and therefore, the coil is used for cooling, i.e., to remove heat.

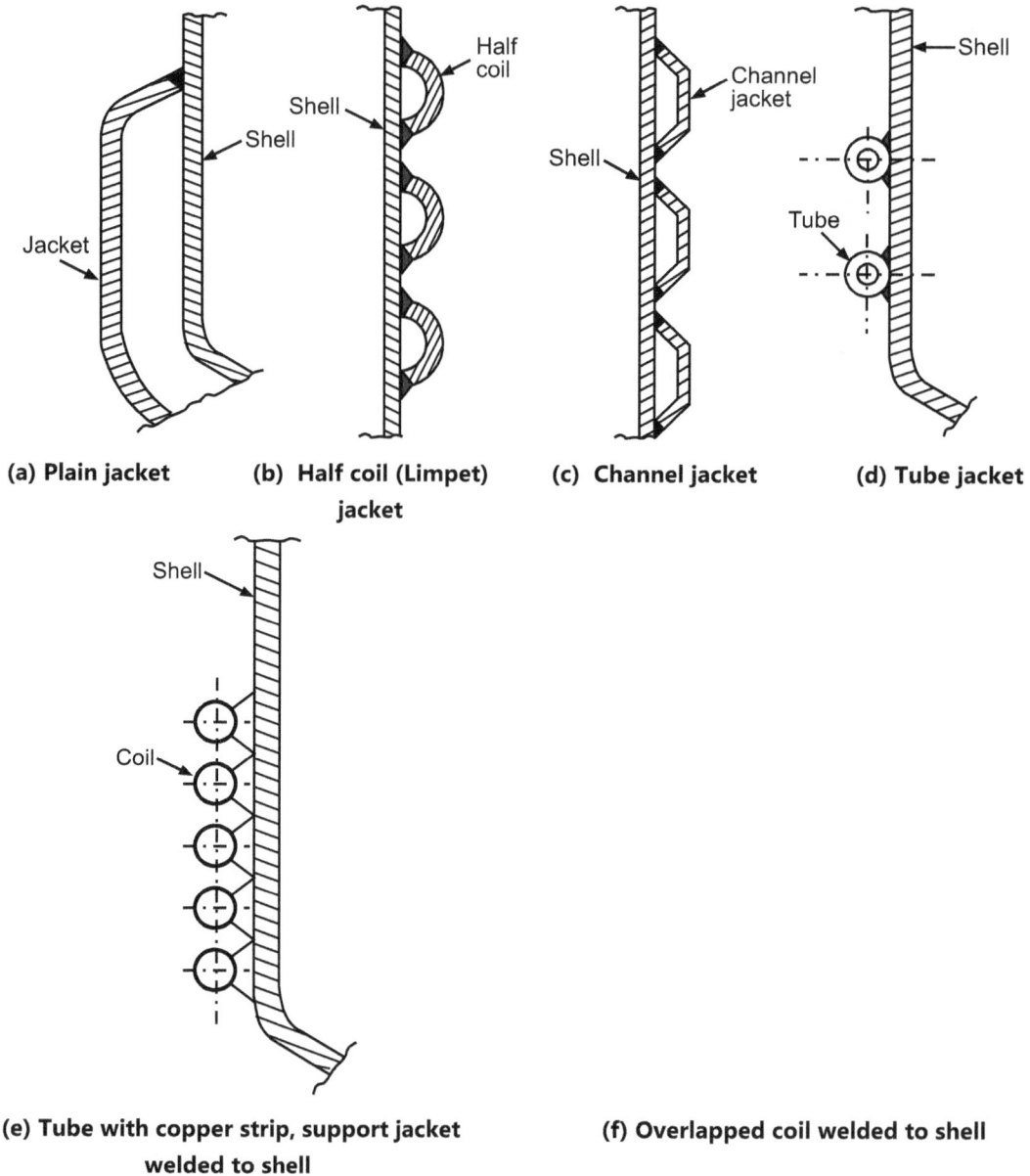

(a) Plain jacket　　(b) Half coil (Limpet)　　(c) Channel jacket　　(d) Tube jacket
jacket

(e) Tube with copper strip, support jacket　　　(f) Overlapped coil welded to shell
welded to shell

Fig. 5.15

Fig. 5.15 shows different types of jackets. A plain jacket is the simplest form of jacket used for heating or cooling and is generally used for steam. Channel and coiled jackets are used to obtain high velocities of circulating fluids. Mild steel is a common material of construction for jackets.

Fig. 5.16 shows different methods of attaching jacket to the vessel wall. Fig. 5.17 shows a method of attaching jacket to the bottom head of the reactor.

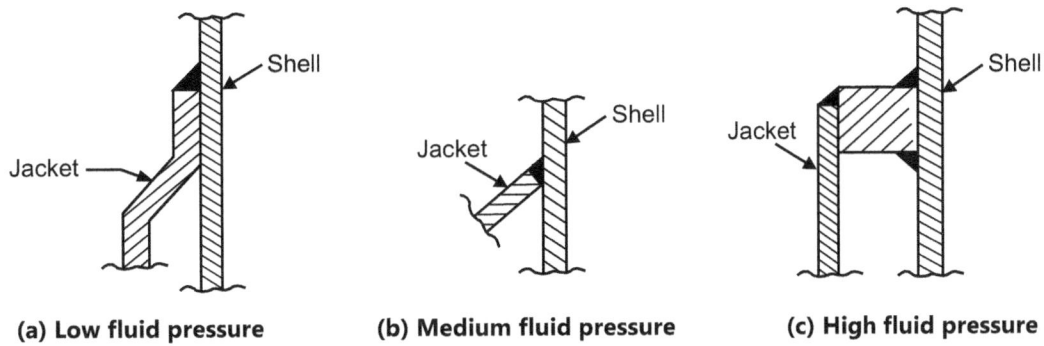

(a) Low fluid pressure   **(b) Medium fluid pressure**   **(c) High fluid pressure**

Fig. 5.16 : Jacket welded to the pressure vessel shell

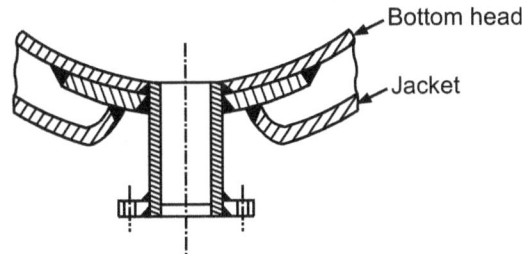

Fig. 5.17 : Bottom outlet nozzle with reinforcing pad welded to head, and jacket welded to pad

Coils are immersed in the contents of the vessel and occupy, a certain volume of the vessel, and make the construction complicated to a certain extent. They may be used for heating or cooling purpose but in the majority cases for cooling. Fig. 5.18 shows various types of coils. The coils are generally formed out of a tubing by shaping them.

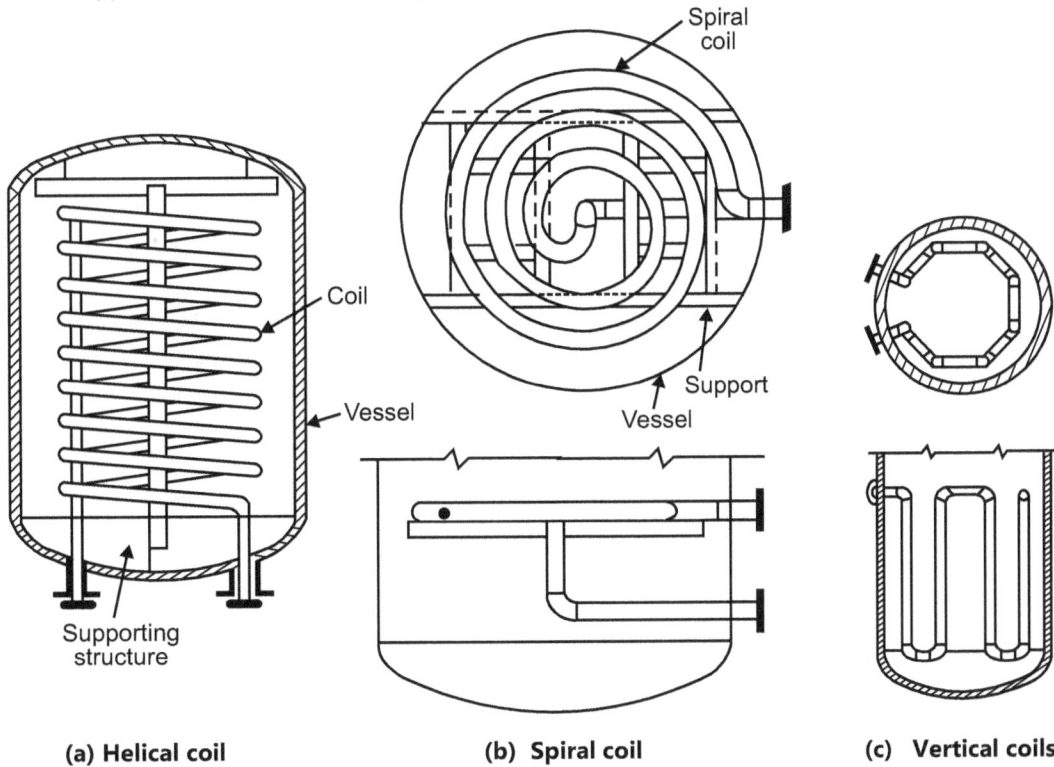

(a) Helical coil   **(b) Spiral coil**   **(c) Vertical coils**

Fig. 5.18 : Coils

5.2.5 Agitators

In the industry, operations such as dissolution, dilution, dispersion, blending, etc. as well some unit processes require agitation of the liquids. In case of batch reactors, semibatch reactors and continuous stirred tank reactors (CSTR) the reactor contents are required to be agitated to enhance both heat and mass transfer. An agitator (also known as a stirrer) produces high velocity liquid streams which moves through the vessel resulting in complete mixing of the contents. The agitator helps to increase the rate of heat transfer and provide an intimate contact of the reacting components by mixing action. Therefore, the composition and temperature are uniform throughout the reaction vessel due to complete mixing.

The main parts of any agitator are the hub and the blades. The hub is attached to the shaft by means of keys or bolts.

Here, we will consider only some of the paddle and turbine agitators.

The blades of paddle agitators normally extend close to the vessel wall. These agitators generally rotate with a low speed and are simply pushers. Highly viscous liquids and pastes are agitated by multiple blade paddles. Generally the paddle diameter is

0.8 times the vessel (inside) diameter and the width of the paddle blades is 1/4th to 1/10th of the paddle diameter. Anchors are used for preventing the formation of deposits on the heat transfer surface as in a reaction vessel and are commonly employed for obtaining improved heat transfer in high viscosity fluids. Paddles cover wide viscosity range and are relatively low in cost.

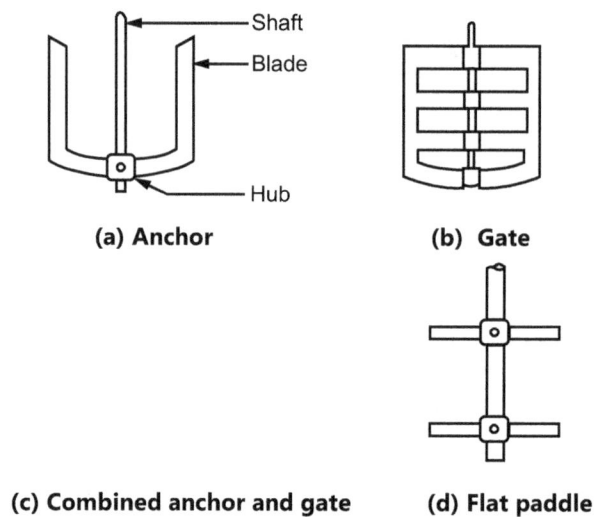

(a) Anchor   (b) Gate

(c) Combined anchor and gate   (d) Flat paddle

Fig. 5.19 : Paddle agitators

Turbine agitators are capable of creating a vigorous mixing action due to centrifugal and rotational motion generated by them. The blades of this agitator may be attached to a central hub or to a central disc. The diameter of the agitator is one-third to one-sixth of the vessel inside diameter. The blade length is one-fourth the agitator diameter. In case of agitators with central disc, the blade length is 1/8th of the agitator diameter. These are high speed agitators compared to the paddles and are very effective over a wide range of viscosities (upto 10^4 cP). A disc flat blade turbine is commonly used in the reaction vessels. Fig. 5.20 shows various types of turbine agitators.

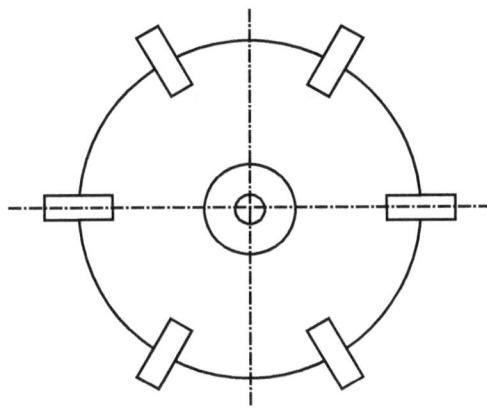

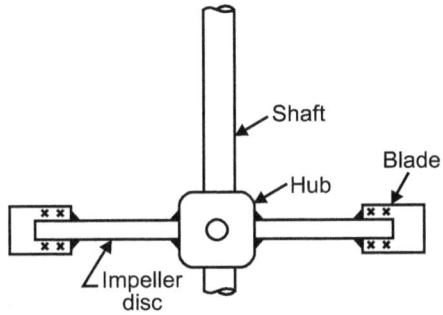

(a) Disc-flat blade turbine

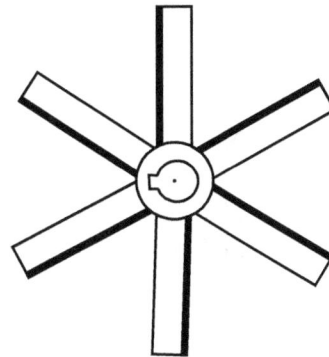

(b) Pitched blade

(c) Straight disc-flat blade turbine agitator (riveted)

Fig. 5.20 : Turbine agitators

5.2.6 Baffles

Use of baffles in vertical vessels is essential for efficient mixing action and minimisation of vortex formation. Baffles are flat vertical strips and mounted against the walls of the vessel. It is a common practice to use four baffles (mounted vertically on the vessel wall, projecting radially from the wall and located 90° apart). The width of the baffle is one-tenth to one-twelfth of the vessel diameter. The baffle height is atleast twice the diameter of agitator and approximately centred on the agitator. The baffles are welded to the straight portion of the vessel.

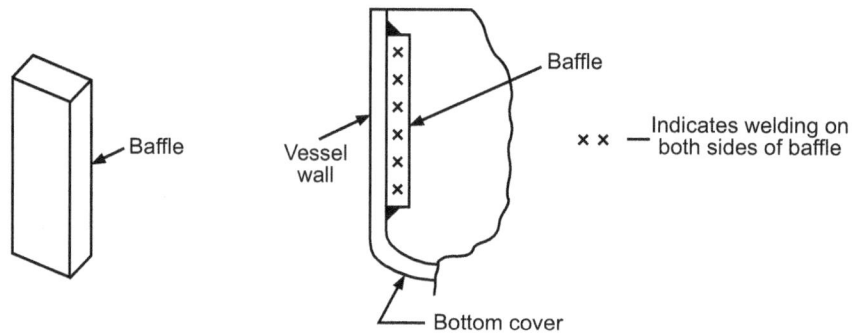

Fig. 5.21 : Baffle

5.2.7 Stuffing Box

A shaft is a rotating, solid (usually) cylindrical piece/member of a certain diameter and length which transmits mechanical power from one point to another point (from a prime mover to an equipment).

Shafts are usually circular in cross-section. The shaft of an agitator is a solid cylindrical piece of a certain diameter and length. Shafts are fabricated from mild steel, stainless steel, etc.

A stuffing box is a part which provides an annular space around the shaft to contain the gland and the gland packing. The stuffing box is attached to the top cover of a reaction vessel through the shaft passes. It is used to center the shaft and to seal the vessel against leakage (it prevents outflow of the fluid from the vessel). Fig. 5.22 shows a stuffing-gland box assembly.

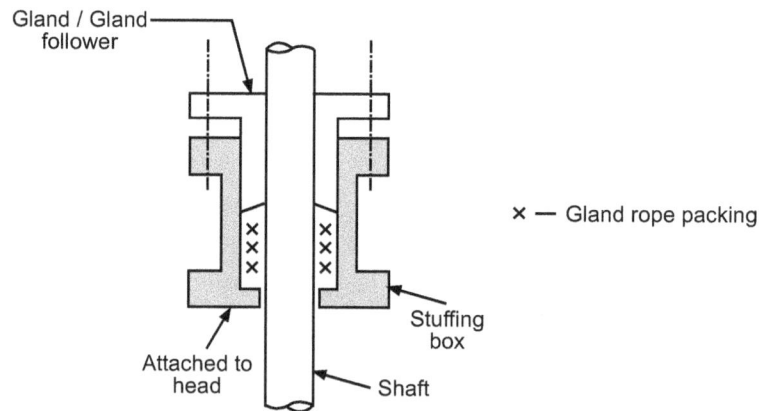

Fig. 5.22 : Stuffing-gland box assembly

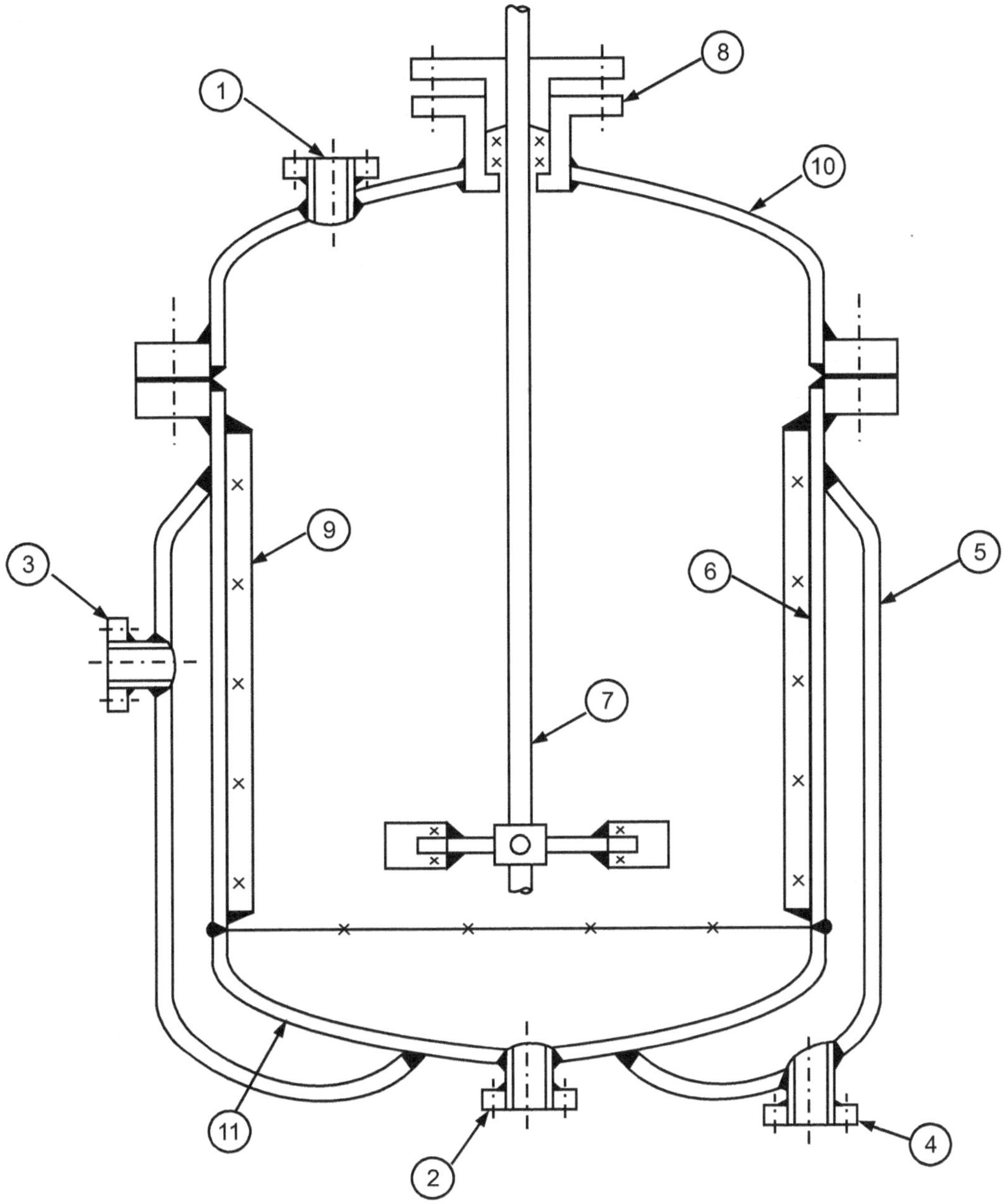

Fig. 5.23 : Jacketed batch or semibatch reactor (Section lines are not shown)

In case of CSTR, a certain pool of the content of the reactor is always maintained in it, so generally the outlet from this reactor is located near the top portion of the shell.

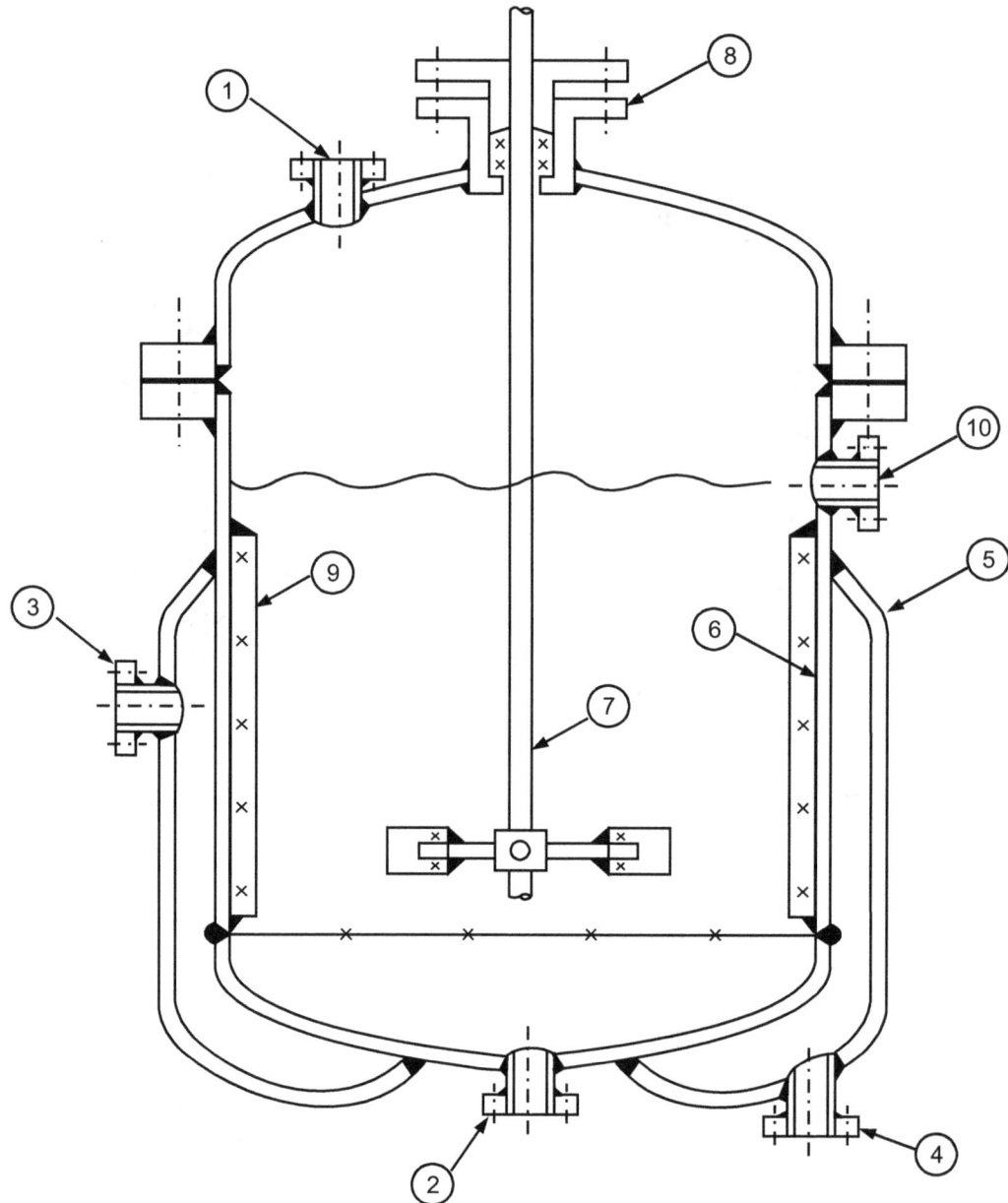

Fig. 5.24 : CSTR (Jacketed)

5.3 HORIZONTAL STORAGE TANKS

Horizontal storage tanks are used in industry for storage of liquid products in relatively small quantities, underground storage of flammable liquids and for intermediate storage of semifinished products in the processing area of a chemical palnt. These are also used for storage of liquid under moderate pressures.

The horizontal storage tanks are cylindrical vessels which consist of a cylindrical shell closed at both the ends by a suitable type of head/closure and are provided with flanged nozzle connections at suitable locations for inlet, outlet, hand hole, man hole, etc. Both the ends or covers are welded to the cylindrical shell by butt welding.

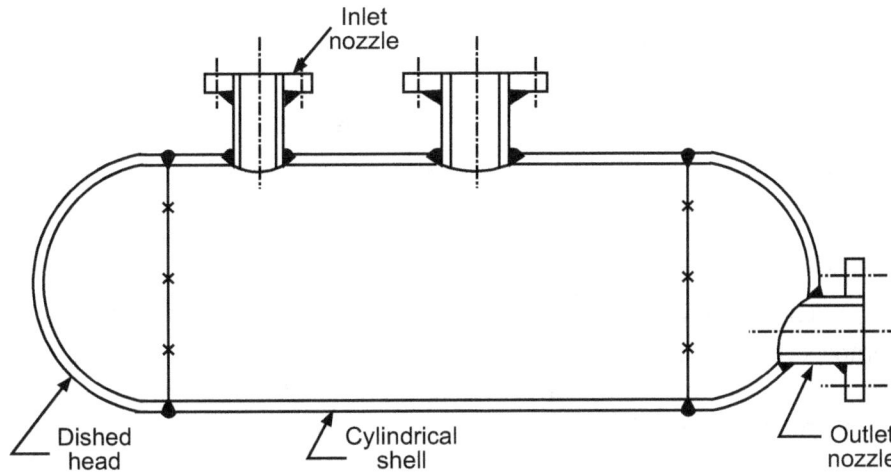

Fig. 5.25 : Horizontal storage tank

5.4 STANDARD VERTICAL SHORT TUBE EVAPORATOR (CALENDRIA TYPE)

In the chemical process industries, evaporators are used for concentration of solutions by evaporation of a part of the solvent (usually water) by thermal means. For this purpose, steam is the most common heating medium used in industry. In most of the evaporators, the heat is transferred through tubular surfaces. The body of an evaporator is in the form of a cylindrical shell in which tubes are incorporated. Standard evaporators usually consist of a vertical tube bundle placed in a vertical cylindrical vessel, known as calendria. These evaporators have a provision for vapour space either as an extension of the calendria or as a separate vessel. Various types of evaporators are jacketed pan, agitated film type evaporator, standard vertical short tube evaporator, horizontal tube evaporator, long tube evaporator, forced circulation evaporator, etc.

This evaporator consists of a large vertical cylindrical vessel. These evaporators of
1 to 6 metre in diameter incorporating a short vertical tube bundle at the bottom portion of the vessel. The tube bundle comprises of tubes of 25 mm to 75 mm outside diameter and
75 cm to 200 cm length. The solution to be concentrated is inside the tubes and heating medium usually steam surrounds the tubes. The tube bundle is held between two tube sheets, which are bolted to shell flanges. A central down take which promotes circulation is of area ranging from 40 to 100% of the total cross-sectional area of the surrounding tubes. The main components of this evaporator are the calendria, evaporator body or vapour release chamber and two dished heads- one at the bottom and the top. Nozzles at appropriate locations are provided for inlet of the solution, vapour outlet, concentrated liquor outlet, steam inlet, condensate outlet, etc. As scaling occurs inside the tubes, this evaporator is used for more rigorous services than the horizontal tube evaporator [Refer Fig. 5.26].

Standard short tube vertical evaporator

(a) drum, (b) calendria, (c) tubes, (d) down-take, (e) steam inlet, (f) condensate outlet, (g) feed (h) tube sheet

Fig. 5.26

5.5 TYPES OF PACKINGS

To obtain an efficient gas-liquid contact (necessary for mass transfer), many different types of packings are available ranging from simple to complex geometrical shapes but are generally classified as random packings and regular packings. If the packings are simply dumped in the tower during installation and the individual pieces are not arranged in any particular pattern, they are known as Random Packings. The packings arranged in a particular pattern are called regular/stacked packings.

In case of randomly packed installations for obtaining high and uniform voidage and prevent breakage, the tower is first filled with liquid usually water and packings are then dumped in it. The most common random packings used in industrial towers are Raschig Rings, Pall Rings, Berl Saddles, Intalox Saddles, etc. Pall rings are made out of metal or plastic (poly propylene) and have the same general form as raschig rings with height equal to diameter, however a part of the original cylinder wall is cut with the projections bend inward leaving holes in the wall. They are generally available in the size ranging from 16 to 50 mm. Berl saddles and Intalox saddles are available in the range 6 to 50 mm and are formed out of plastic or ceramics.

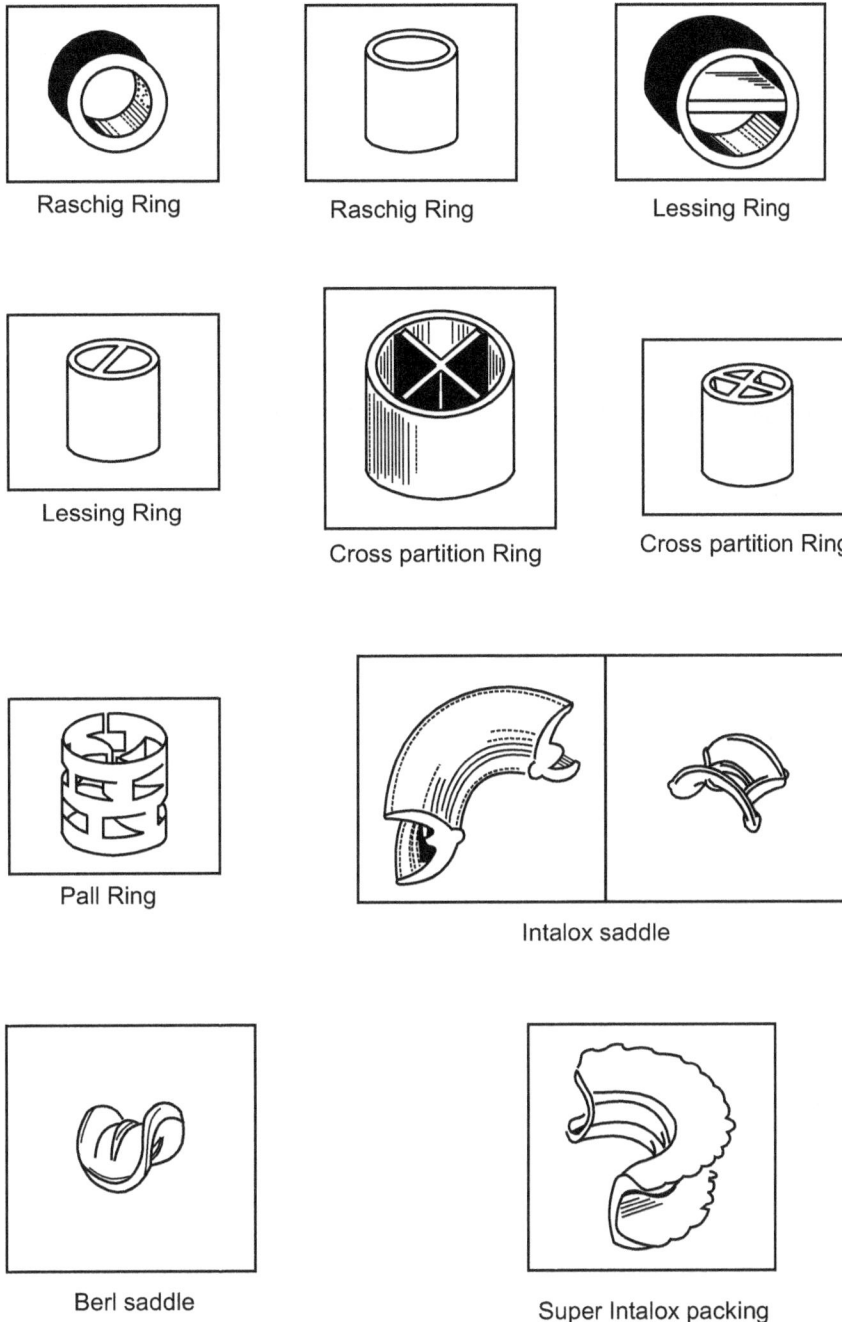

Raschig Ring   Raschig Ring   Lessing Ring

Lessing Ring   Cross partition Ring   Cross partition Ring

Pall Ring   Intalox saddle

Berl saddle   Super Intalox packing

Fig. 5.27 : Packings

Raschig rings are hollow cylinders with their length equal to the outside diameter and usually formed out of ceramic, carbon or metal. They are generally available in sizes from 6 to 100 mm. When a single web is added to the inside of Raschig ring, we get Lessing ring and when a cross web is added to the Raschig ring, we get what is known as Partion ring. They are normally available in sizes from 75 to 150 mm and usually as Regular/stacked packings. Stacked packings offer lower pressure drop than random packings for equivalent phase flow rates.

Packings are gas-liquid contacting devices. Packings are supported in the column over suitable packing supports. Packed columns are particularly useful in case of vacuum distillation and in gas absorption.

5.6 LIQUID DISTRIBUTORS

A liquid distributor is a device that spreads a liquid uniformly across the top of the packing. Several types of liquid distributors are used for the said purpose. For small diameter columns, weir type liquid distributors are used and for large diameter columns spinder type (a spider pipe with multiple arms) liquid distributors are used.

(a) **Weir-type liquid distributor**   (b) **Spider type liquid distributor**

Fig. 5.28

5.7 LIQUID REDISTRIBUTOR

Fig. 5.29 : Liquid redistributor

The liquid moving down the column has a tendency to drift towards the wall although of it is efficiently distributed at the top of packings and hence after a certain downward vertical height of liquid travel, liquid concentration drops considerably in the inner cross-section. Therefore, it is necessary to direct the liquid towards the centre of the column after it has travelled a certain distance. For this the packing height (packed bed) is divided into more than one section and a liquid redistributor is provided between two packing sections.

5.8 GRID BAR SUPPORT PLATE

Grid bar support plate is located at the bottom of the column and supports the packings. It is a conventional type of support plate in which free area is limited to 30 to 40%.

Fig. 5.30 : Grid bar support plate

5.9 TYPES OF HEADS OR COVERS

Processing equipments such as distillation columns, absorbers, heat exchangers, reactors are essentially cylindrical closed vessels with formed heads of one type or another.

For closing either end of the cylindrical shell, a cover or a closure is necessary. The closure/head can be attached to the shell by welding, riveting or bolting technique. The simplest cover is a flat plate of the diameter same as that of the shell. The flat closures are used as manhole covers and for small bore openings, these are used for low pressure service. The closures formed to specific shapes are known as formed heads. The plain formed head (Fig. 5.31) is produced by simply forming a straight flange with a radius on a flat plate. These are used mainly for closing the ends of horizontal cylindrical storage vessels at atmospheric pressure that store fuel oil, kerosene, and miscellaneous liquids having low vapour pressures. They are also used as the bottom heads of vertical cylindrical vessels that rest on concrete slabs. The flat portion of such heads can be dished to form flanged and dished heads. The pressure rating of flanged only head/plain formed head is increased by dishing their flat portion. The dished heads consist of two radii – the crow radius or radius of dish and the inside corner radius (known as the knuckle radius).

On the basis of the depth of dishing and its shape, these heads are classified as shallow dished, flared and dished, torispherical, elliptical, hemispherical and conical. Flared and shallow dished heads are used for low pressure service. Torispherical dished heads are used for pressure upto 15 kgf/cm^2. Elliptical heads are used for pressures above 15 kgf/cm^2. For a given thickness, hemispherical heads are the strongest of the formed heads but are expensive. To facilitate removal or draining of material, conical heads are used.

If the crown radius is greater than the shell outside diameter, the head is known as a flanged and shallow dished head. If the crown radius is equal to the shell outside diameter, the head is known as a standard dished head. If the crown radius is less than the shell outside diameter, the head is known as flanged and torispherical dished head.

While drawing a shallow dished head, take the crown radius 10% greater than the outside diameter of the head. For a standard dished head take the crown radius equal to the outside diameter and for a torispherical dished head, take the crown radius 10% less than the outside diameter of head. For an elliptical head, take the ratio of major to minor axis equal to two. In case of conical heads, an apex angle of 60° is provided and are used as bottom heads for equipments such as crystallisers, evaporators and spray driers to facilitate removal of materials (solids) from such equipments. The inside corner radius is 6% of the inside diameter for heads other than the conical head for which it is 10% of the inside diameter of head or shell. The length of the straight flange portion on the head is atleast three times the head thickness with minimum of 20 mm.

For drawing of heads on drawing sheet, use following dimensions :

UD = 80 mm, t = 2 to 3 mm, S_f = 20 mm., Inside corner radius - icr = 5 to 6 mm.

For conical head - icr = 8 mm., For shallow dished head crown radius - C_r = 90 mm.

For standard dished head - C_r = 80 mm., For torispherical dished head – C_r = 70 mm.

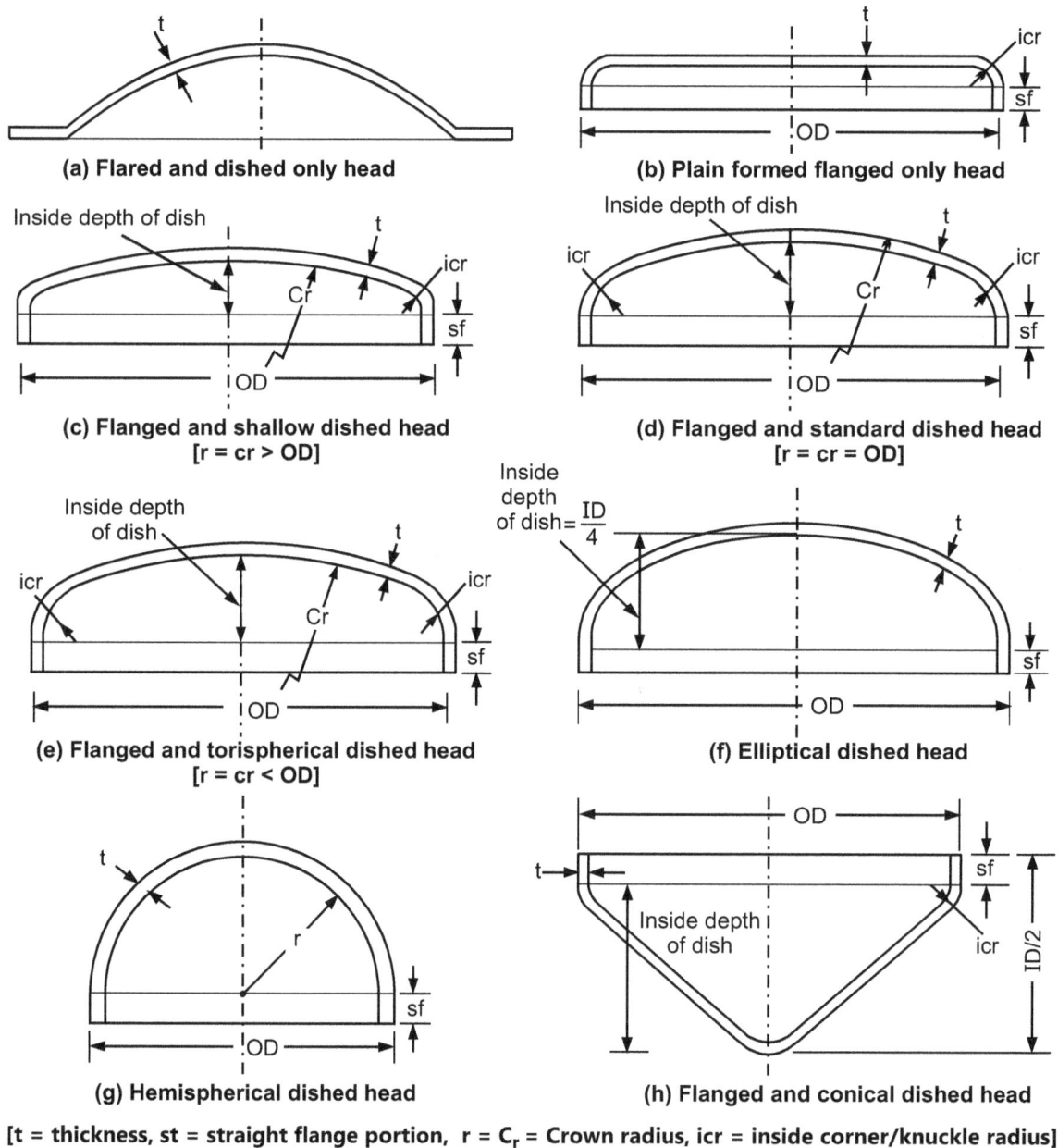

(a) Flared and dished only head

(b) Plain formed flanged only head

(c) Flanged and shallow dished head
[r = cr > OD]

(d) Flanged and standard dished head
[r = cr = OD]

(e) Flanged and torispherical dished head
[r = cr < OD]

(f) Elliptical dished head

(g) Hemispherical dished head

(h) Flanged and conical dished head

[t = thickness, st = straight flange portion, r = C$_r$ = Crown radius, icr = inside corner/knuckle radius]

Fig. 5.31 : Types of heads/covers

Attachment of Head and Shell

Heads are attached to the shell by a welded or a flange joint. In the case of welded joint, either a lap or butt construction is made depending upon the thickness of the shell and head.

Fig. 5.33 shows welded joints. Flanged joints are datachable, unlike the welded joints which are permanent.

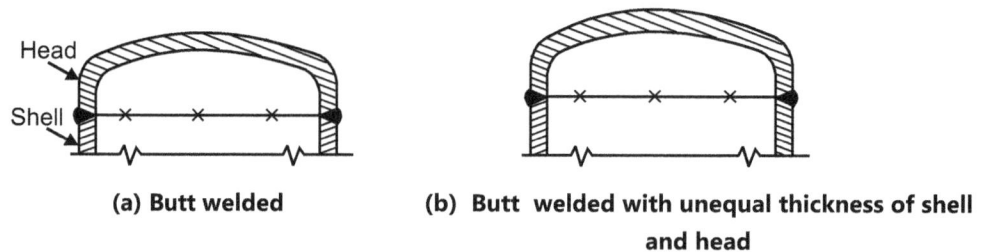

(a) Butt welded

(b) Butt welded with unequal thickness of shell and head

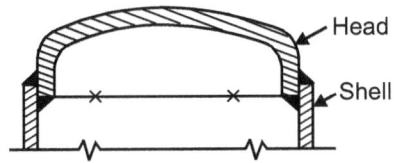

(c) Lap welded

Fig. 5.32 : Attachment of formed heads to shell

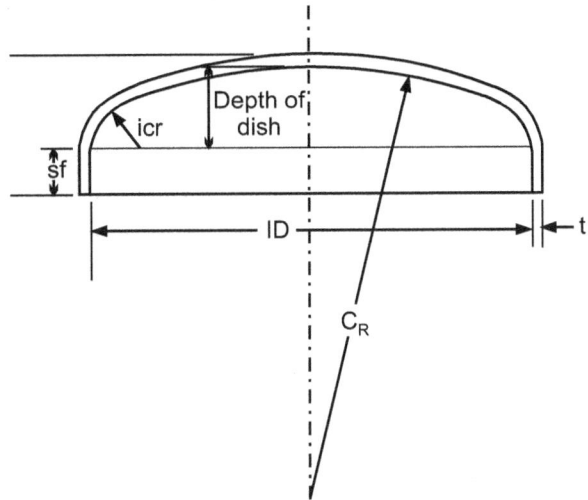

Fig. 5.33 : Flanged and dished head (shallow/standard/torispherical)

● ● ●

SPECIFICATION SHEET

After listing the required equipments, transportation devices, etc. from engineering flow sheets and making necessary design calculations, we have to prepare a specification form/specification sheet for each piece of equipment/device. The specification form/sheet serves as both a request form by the purchaser and a final bid form by the supplier. This sheet contains all information deemed essential such as materials handled, capacity, operating conditions, construction and material details, etc. The writing of specifications is a requisite of every chemical engineer.

6.1 SPECIFICATION SHEET FOR CENTRIFUGAL PUMP

1.	Specification No. .... Date ....
2.	Number required .... Working stand-by
3.	Operation Parallel/Continuous/Intermittent location ....
4.	Operating conditions
5.	Fluid pumped .... composition ....
6.	Density .... Viscosity .... pH ....
7.	Working temperature .... Vapour pressure ....
8.	Flow rate/capacity Min .... Normal .... Maximum ....
9.	Pressure : Suction .... Discharge ....
10.	NPSH .... Total head ....
11.	Pump construction
12.	Casing .... Seal/gland type ....
13.	Thrust bearing type .... Journal bearing type ....
14.	No. of stages .... Type ....
15.	Speed .... Drive torque ....
16.	Size inlet .... Size discharge .... Size drain ....
17.	Materials of construction.
18.	Casing .... Impeller ....
19.	Shaft .... Shaft sleeve .... Neck bush (shaft) ....
20.	Gland packing/seal .... Thrust bearing ....
21.	Gland sleeve .... Mounting ....
22.	Drive details
23.	Drive type .... Speed ratio ....
24.	Coupling type .... Guard type ....

25.	Motor : HP .... Volts .... Phase .... Cycles ....
	type .... rpm .... class ....
26.	Design code .... Weight ....
27.	Design pressure .... Hydrostatic test pressure
	Prepared by .... Checked by .... Approved by ....
	Name of party and Address ....

e.g. Specification No. : CP 1001

6.2 SPECIFICATION SHEET FOR HEAT EXCHANGER

		Shell side	Tube side
1.	Specification No. .... Date		
2.	Number required .... Location		
3.	Type .... Duty as		
4.	Operating data/conditions		
5.	Fluid description	Shell side	Tube side
6.	Name	In ... out ...	In ... out ...
7.	Composition	In ... out ...	In ... out ...
8.	Flow rate, kg/h	In ... out ...	In ... out ...
9.	Density, kg/m^3	In ... out ...	In ... out ...
10.	Viscosity, cP	In ... out ...	In ... out ...
11.	Specific heat,	....	....
12.	Latent heat, kcal/kg	....	....
13.	Thermal conductivity	....	....
14.	Temperature, ºC	In ... out ...	In ... out ...
15.	Operating pressure, kgf/cm^2·g	In ... out ...	In ... out ...
16.	No. of passes	....	....
17.	Velocity, m/s	....	....
18.	Fouling resistance	....	....
19.	Heat exchange duty ...... kcal/kg LMTD ...... ºC		
20.	Overall heat transfer coefficient .... kcal/m^2·h·ºC.		
21.	Tube : OD ...... mm, length ...... m, wall thickness (BWG)		
	pitch ...... mm □ Δ material		
22.	Shell : Nom. OD ...... length ...... mm thickness		
23.	Shell cover : ...... Material		
24.	Channel ...... Channel cover		
25.	Tube sheet type ...... (stationary/floating)		
26.	Baffles : type ...... No. ...... Thickness		
27.	Shell side nozzles : Inlet ...... outlet ...... drain		

28.	Tube side nozzles : Inlet ...... outlet ......
29.	Corrosion allowance : shell side ...... tube side ......
30.	Gaskets ....
31.	Design code ....
32.	Design pressure and temperature ... kgf/cm²·g, ... °C ... kgf/cm²·g, ... °C
33.	Test pressure and temperature ......, ... , ..., ...
34.	Weight : Dry ......, Tube bundle ...... Unit full of water ...... kg.
35.	Remarks ....
	Prepared by ...... Checked by ...... Approved by ...... Name and Address ....

6.3 SPECIFICATION SHEET FOR BATCH REACTOR (JACKETED)

1.	Specification No. .... Date ....
2.	Number required .... Location ....
3.	Capacity (volumetric) ....
4.	Operating conditions
5.	Process materials handled ....
6.	Feed composition .... density .... viscosity ....
7.	Product mix. composition .... density .... viscosity ....
8.	Temperature .... Pressure ....
9.	Construction details
10.	Reactor shell : dia. .... height .... thickness ....
11.	Heads type ....
12.	Jacket heating surface .... Pressure on Jacket side ....
13.	Jacket : type ....
14.	Jacket : length .... dia. .... thickness ....
15.	Vessel connections :
16.	Inlet : No. .... size Outlet : No. .... size ....
17.	Manhole size .... Stuffing box opening ....
18.	Pressure gauge connection .... Thermowell pocket ....
19.	Jacket connections :
20.	Steam inlet .... condensate size ....
21.	Water inlet ....water outlet .... jacket drain ....
22.	Agitator type .... Agitator/impeller dia. ....
23.	Speed ....
24.	Shaft : dia. .... length ....
25.	Blades : No. .... width .... breadth .... thickness ....

26.	Baffles : No. .... length .... width ....
27.	Stuffing box : Make .... type .... gaskets ....
28.	Special fittings : Relief valve ....
29.	Materials of construction
30.	Vessel .... Jacket .... Agitator ....
31.	Vessel nozzles .... Jacket nozzles ....
32.	Drive details
33.	Drive : type .... gear ratio .... arrangement (V/H) ....
34.	Motor : type .... HP .... phase .... cycles .... rpm .... class
35.	Design code .... Design pressure ....
36.	Hydrostatic test pressure ....
37.	Weight : dry .... unit full of water ....
38.	Services required :
39.	Steam : pressure .... flow ....
40.	Cooling water : Maximum temperature .... flow ....
41.	Support : type ....No. .... Bracket size ....
42.	Column support for bracket : size ....
43.	Remarks ....
	Prepared by .... Checked by .... Approved by .... Name and Address ....

●●●

FLOW SHEETING

- The flow sheet is the road map of a process.
- It is a diagrammatic model of the process.

7.1 TYPES OF FLOW SHEETS/FLOW DIAGRAMS

(i)   Block diagram or block type flow sheet.

(ii)   Process flow sheet/process flow diagram.

(iii)   Piping and instrumentation diagram.

(iv)   Utility flow sheet/diagram or utility line diagram.

(v)   Piping plans and installation diagrams.

7.1.1 Block Diagram

A block diagram is the simplest form of presentation of a process. In this diagram, each piece of equipment or a complete stage in the process is shown by a rectangular box/block and equipment or operation designation should be indicated within the block. The rectangular boxes/blocks representing the steps involved are joined to each other in proper sequence by arrows which represent the streams that go between the blocks/boxes – i.e., the streams entering and leaving each block - each step. The information regarding a stream (material, stream conditions, etc.) entering/leaving a block should be shown on an arrow representing the stream.

Block diagrams are used to set forth a preliminary or basic processing concept without details. They are useful for representing a process in a simplified form in reports and textbooks, and showing material and energy balances around a part of the process or over the entire process. Also used in research summaries and process proposals.

In such diagrams, the blocks should be drawn using thick lines and arrows should be drawn using thin lines.

7.1.2 Process Flow Sheet/Process Flow Diagram

A process flow sheet or process flow diagram is one which depicts the process equipments together with the flow routes from raw material feed to final product.

Process flow diagrams show the functioning of the process, depicting all its essential parts and connections by means of symbols arranged to show the operation without regard to physical layout of various items, their parts or connection.

The process flow sheet/process flow diagram shows the arrangement of the equipments needed to carry out the process and their interconnection.

A process flow sheet includes :

(i)   All process equipments.

(ii)   Utilities to perform various operations. The utilities required are to be shown by labelled arrows – i.e., by utility connections (e.g., steam).

(iii)   Flow rates or quantity of each stream.

(iv)   Stream material and composition of each stream.

(v)   Operating conditions of each stream and equipment, such as temperature and pressure.

(vi)   Symbolic representation of a hazard, safety precautions, etc.

The process flow diagram is a very useful diagram in the chemical industry.

(i)   It effectively communicates the design information.

(ii)   It helps the operator for adjusting process parameters.

(iii)   It helps the supervisor in checking and controlling the plant operation.

(iv)   It will be used as the basis for developing other diagrams.

(v)   It is used for comparison and evaluation of different processes by the project engineers.

Chemical engineers always refer to this diagram to show the sequence of operations and equipments in the process as this diagram gives idea regarding operations performed on the raw materials in a correct sequence from raw material feed to finished product.

In the process flow sheet every equipment, vessel, machinery, etc. is shown by a suitable symbol (for reducing detailed description on it.)

In this book for symbolic representation of equipments, machineries, etc. we are making use of Graphical Symbols as per **IS : 3232 – 1976**.

Points to be kept in mind while drawing a process flow sheet :

1.   Use symbols as per IS : 3232 - 1976.

2.   Draw every symbol to appropriate size.

3.   No need to draw this diagram floor wise.

4.   No need to show storage tanks for raw materials and finished product(s). No transfer means-pumps, etc. are required to be shown.

5.   Symbols and process lines should be drawn thick and all other lines should be drawn thin.

6.   The utilities (service connections) required for each individual operation should be shown by arrows and labelled. No need to show the utility header lines.

7.   Arrangement of the diagram should be in accordance with the sequence of flow of material. The diagram should be drawn preferably left to right.

8.   As far as possible, parts of the diagram should be evenly spaced.

9.   The diagram should not be too zig-zag in appearance.

10.   The diagram should be drawn as far as possible with connections in straight perpendicular lines with minimum number of cross over.

11.   Legend comprising of code and description [i.e., the key to the code-equipment key] should be prepared at the top right hand side of the drawing sheet.

12.   Use upper case/capital letters for writing text on the diagram.

13.   Title should be given at the bottom of the diagram in such a way that it will appear as far as possible centrally of the diagram.

14.   The arrows (indicating the direction of flow) are to be drawn on every line at the end of the line.

15.   No pipe fittings/valves are required to be shown.

Equipment identification :

Every equipment on the flow sheet should be identified by a equipment code. The equipment code should be written within the flow sheet symbol representing equipment and if possible it may be encircled. The easiest code is to use an initial letter to identify the type of equipment, followed by digits to identify the particular piece. The codes are not standard and one can make use of one, two or at the most three alpha-bets from the name of the equipment. The code numbering is to be done from left to right in increasing order whenever there is a repetition of the same type of equipment on the flow sheet. [e.g. for two batch reactor in series – BR-1 for the first reactor and BR-2 for the second reactor (from left of the drawing sheet)].

The key to the code [i.e., Equipment key/legend comprising of - equipment code and description in a tabular form] should be shown on the flow sheet (as far as possible at the top of the RHS of the drawing sheet).

For example :

Name of equipment	Equipment code
Reactor	R-1
Batch reactor	BR-1
Heat exchanger	HE-1
Distillation columns (2 Nos)	DC-1, DC-2
Absorption towers (2 Nos)	AT-1, AT-2
Pumps (3 Nos)	P-1, P-2, P-3
Heater	H-1
Condenser	CON-1

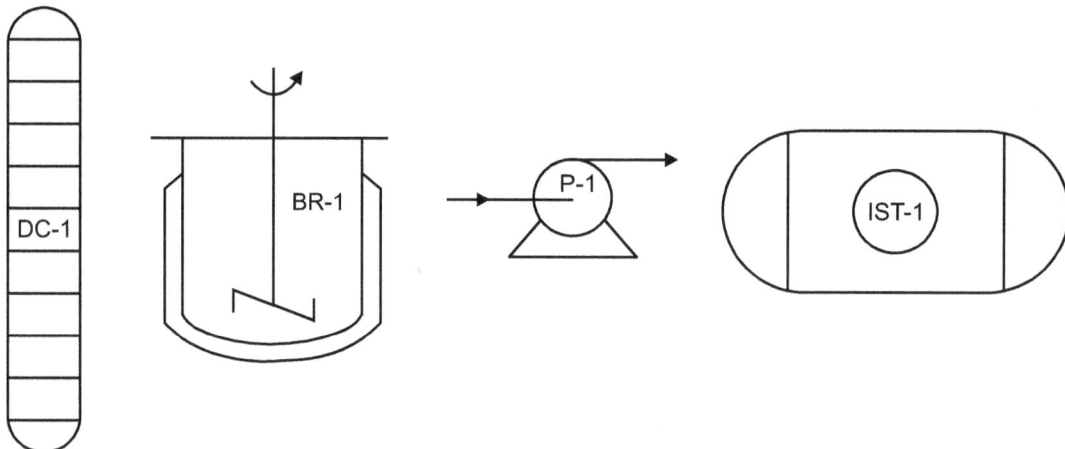

Fig. 7.1 : Equipment coding

Presentation of material flow, stream flow rates, etc.

There are various ways of presentation of data on the process flow sheet.

1.   The material flow indication from one process equipment to another is done as follows :

Assume that a part of the process description is : The slurry containing ortho nitro aniline (ONA) from a batch reactor is fed to a centrifuge where the wet ONA is obtained.

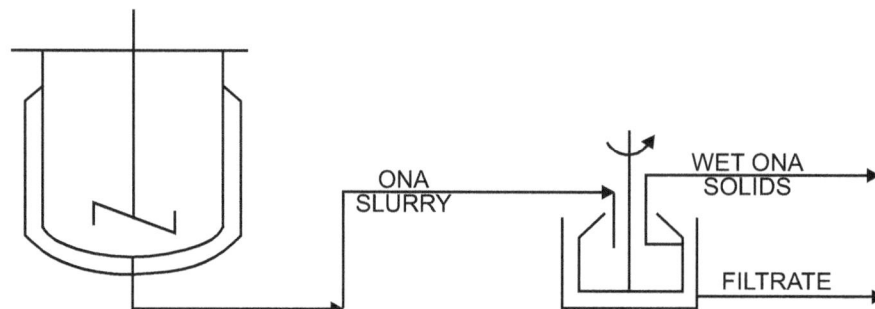

Fig. 7.2 : Material flow indication

2. The inflow line symbol is used for raw materials and outflow line symbol is used for product. For example, if benzene and nitric acid are the raw materials and nitrobenzene is the product of the process then they are indicated on the process flow sheet as :

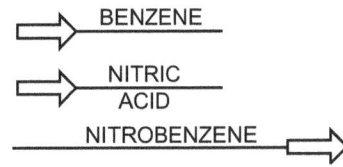

BENZENE

NITRIC ACID

NITROBENZENE

Fig. 7.3 : Raw material, product indication

3. **Process parameters/stream conditions indication** (if provided) of a particular stream on the flow sheet may be done on a line representing the stream consideration. Following example will clear this.

Assume that a part of the process description is : Feed to a fractionating column contains 41 mole % benzene at a temperature of 95° C and is fed at a rate of 1500 kg/h. Plate column is used for the separation of benzene-toluene liquid mixture.

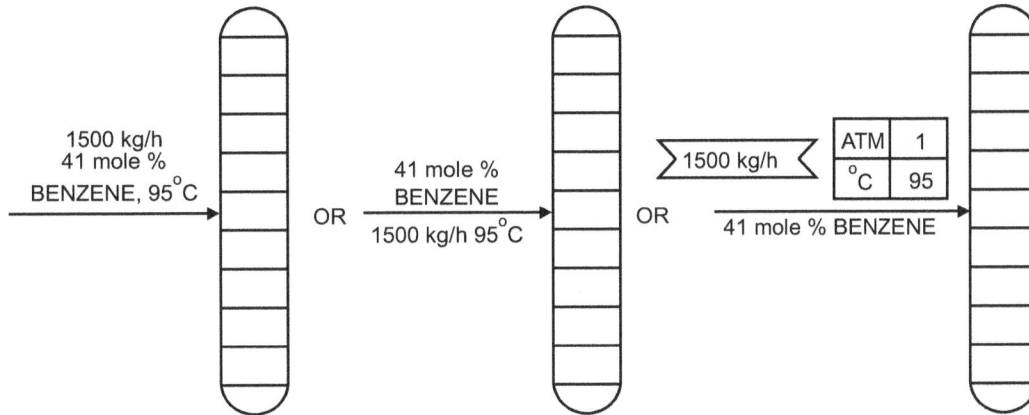

1500 kg/h
41 mole %
BENZENE, 95°C

OR

41 mole %
BENZENE
1500 kg/h 95°C

OR

1500 kg/h

| ATM | 1 |
| °C | 95 |

41 mole % BENZENE

Fig. 7.4 : Stream parameter/stream condition indication

4. Process parameters (process conditions) indication of a particular operation may be done inside the flow sheet symbol representing the operation under consideration. The following example will clear this point.

Example-part of process description : The batch reactor used for ammination reaction operates at a temperature of 160°C and at a pressure of 35 atmosphere, for producing orthonitroaniline from orthonitro-chlorobenzene.

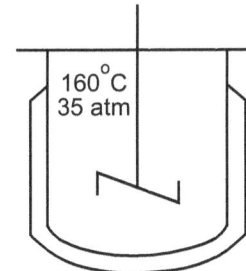

160°C
35 atm

Fig. 7.5 : Equipment condition indication

5. The indication of utilities needed for carrying out a particular operation involved in the process will be clear by referring the following example.

Example - part of process description : A vapour stream leaving distillation column is fed to condenser where it is liquefied by heat exchanger with chilled water.

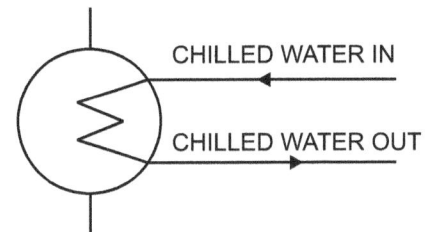

CHILLED WATER IN

CHILLED WATER OUT

Fig. 7.6 : Utility (service) indication

Ex. 7.1 : Benzene sulphonic acid is to be prepared on a continuous basis by sulphonation of benzene. Sulphuric acid is continuously pumped from a storage tank to a sulphonator (jacketed and agitated type – CSTR). The steam heating is required to the sulphonator. Liquid benzene is continuously pumped from the storage tank to a vaporiser (for which steam is used as utility) where it is converted into superheated vapour. Part of benzene vapours are fed to the sulphonator and the remaining part of benzene vapours are fed to a sulphonator tower (plate column) from bottom. In the sulphonator, benzene reacts with sulphuric acid, and the reaction mass containing 30% sulphuric acid (unreacted) from the sulphonator is fed continuously to the top of the sulphonation tower. The reaction mass flows in the downward direction through the tower while doing so it further reacts with benzene vapour rising through the column. The benzene-water vapour mixture from the top of the tower is fed to a condenser and then to a separator. Benzene from separator is then returned to the benzene vaporiser. The product benzene sulphonic acid containing small amounts of sulphone, sulphuric acid is continuously removed from the bottom of the tower. Sulphonation is carried at a temperature of 160 – 180 °C.

(i)   Draw the block diagram of this plant.

(ii)   Draw the process flow sheet/flow diagram of this plant.

Sol. : Now, we will draw the block diagram first and then we will draw the process flow sheet/flow diagram based upon the process description given.

A chemical process comprises of a number of operations in which physical or chemical changes occur. So first list the operations and process equipments used in the process in proper order. One has to read the given process description for two-three times to get a clear idea regarding equipments involved, material flow, sequence of operations, etc.

List of operations and equipments used :

(i)   Vaporisation – vaporiser.

(ii)   Sulphonation – sulphonator (reactor - CSTR).

(iii)   Sulphonation by stage contact – sulphonation tower (like plate column).

(iv)   Condensation – condenser.

(v)   Phase separation – separator/decanter.

List of raw materials required :

(i)   Benzene (liquid)

(ii)   Sulphuric acid (liquid)

List of finished products :

(i)   Benzene sulphonic acid :

Flow of Materials in the Process :

1.   Vaporiser : Input to vaporiser : liquid benzene.

Output from vaporiser : superheated benzene vapour (superheated vapour is a vapour heated beyond saturated temperature).

2.   Sulphonator :

Input to sulphonator :

(i)   Sulphuric acid

(ii)   Part of superheated benzene vapour from vaporiser

Output from sulphonator :

(i)   Benzene + water vapours (to condenser)

(ii)   Product/reaction mass (to tower)

3.   Sulphonation tower :

Input : (i)   Product/reaction mass (from sulphonator)

         (ii)   Benzene vapours (from vaporiser – part of vapour stream)

Output : (i)   Product benzene sulphonic acid (from bottom)

         (ii)   (Benzene + water) vapours (from top)

4.   Condenser :

Input :   (i)   (Benzene + water) vapours (from tower and reactor)

Output : (ii)   Liquid benzene + water i.e. two phase mixture of benzene and water.

5.   Separator / Decanter :

Input :   Two phase liquid mixture (benzene + water) from condenser.

Output : (i)   Liquid water (from bottom)

         (ii)   Liquid benzene (from top).

Sulphuric acid flows from the sulphuric acid storage to the sulphonator. Benzene flows from the storage tank to the vaporiser and then as a vapour from the vaporiser to
(i) sulphonator and (ii) sulphonation tower. Product mass with unreacted sulphuric acid flows from near the top from the sulphonator to the sulphonation tower and benzene in vapour form flows from sulphonation tower to condenser. Benzene sulphonic acid product is removed from the bottom of sulphonation tower, and a mixture of benzene and water flows from the top of sulphonation tower to the condenser. A two phase liquid mixture flows from the condenser to the separator wherein water and benzene are separated and removed separately.

So knowing the flow of materials, we can easily draw the block diagram and process flow diagram. In a block diagram, each equipment or operation is represented by a rectangular block and in process flow diagram/flow sheet, we have to use flow sheet symbols of the equipments involved to represent them.

In both the diagrams, it is not necessary to show storage tanks for raw materials and finished products.

In our case, benzene vapours are introduced into the reactor with the help of a sparger.
A sparger is a device that is used to introduce vapour or gas stream into a pool of liquid in the form of fine bubbles.

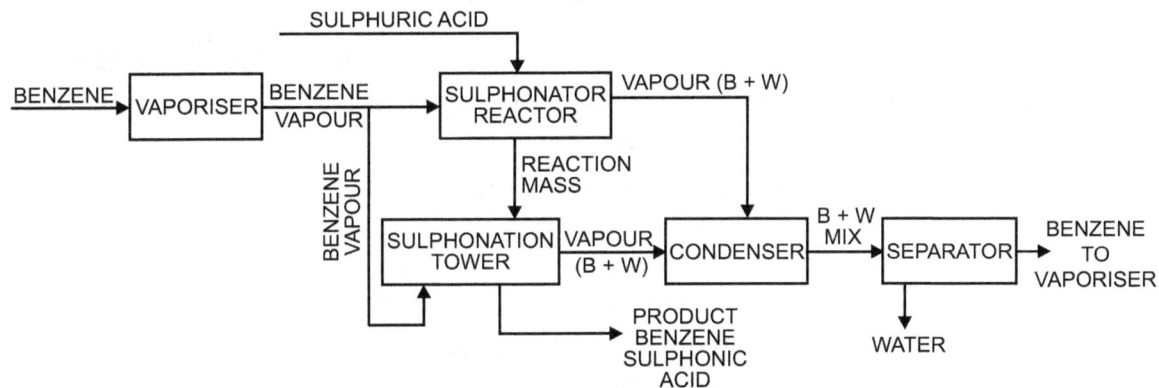

FIG. 7.7 : BLOCK DIAGRAM FOR MANUFACTURE OF BENZENE SULPHONIC ACID BY SULPHONATION OF BENZENE

LEGEND / EQUIPMENT KEY

CODE	DESCRIPTION
V-1	VAPORISER
S-1	SULPHONATOR
SLT-1	SULPHONATION TOWER
CON-1	CONDENSER
SP-1	SEPARATOR

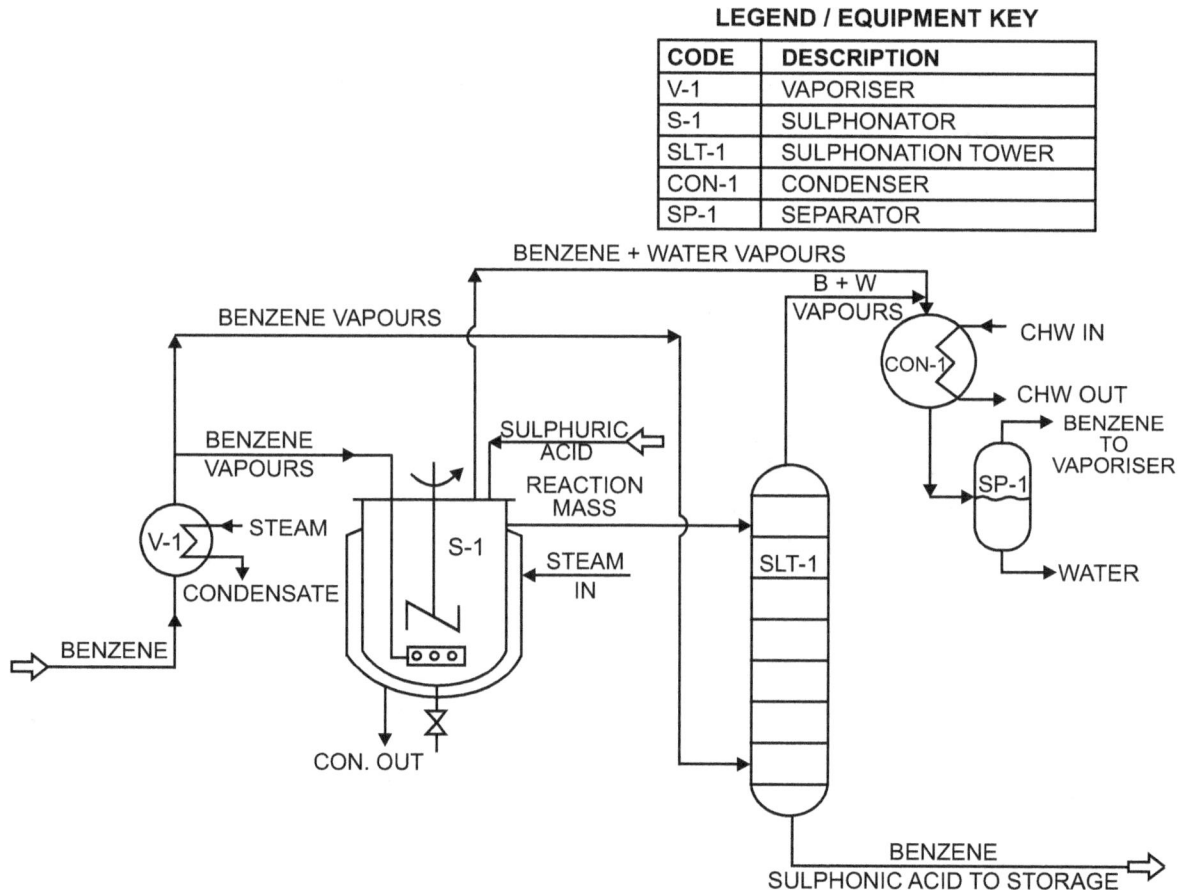

FIG. 7.8 : PROCESS FLOW SHEET/FLOW DIAGRAM FOR PRODUCTION OF BENZENE SULPHONIC ACID BY SULPHONATION OF BENZENE

Ex. 7.2 : Sulphuric acid of commercial grade (98% strength) is to be produced by contact process. Sulphur is the main raw material. In the process, fresh air is fed continuously to a air drying tower with the help of an air blower. Molten sulphur (sulphur in liquid state form) and dried air are fed to a sulphur burner wherein sulphur is oxidised to sulphur dioxide (it is a combustion reaction). The burner outlet gases containing 8 to 10% SO_2 are then cooled in a waste heat boiler from 1000 °C to 450 °C and are then introduced into a catalytic converter (fixed bed catalytic reactor) employing vanadium pentoxide catalyst. In the converter, SO_2 gets oxidised to SO_3 at about 450 °C. The oxidation is exothermic and heat evolved during the course of reaction may be removed by using water to generate steam. The product gas containing SO_3 from the converter is then cooled in a heat exchanger followed by a cooler and then fed to an absorber where SO_3 is absorbed in ~ 97% sulphuric acid. Sulphuric acid itself is used as a absorbent. The acid, leaving the absorber, of 98% strength is then cooled in a double pipe type chiller and finally goes to an intermediate storage tank from which the product sulphuric acid is sent to a bulk storage. The acid of 98% strength from the intermediate storage tank is fed to the air drying tower for drying air. The acid of strength ~ 97% from the drying tower is fed to the absorber for absorption of SO_3.

Burner reaction : $S + O_2 \rightarrow SO_2$, O_2 from air

Converter reaction : $2\,SO_2 + O_2 \longrightarrow 2\,SO_3$

Absorber reaction : $SO_3 + mH_2SO_4 + H_2O \longrightarrow (m + 1)\,H_2SO_4$.

[Here DCDA – double contact double absorption process of sulphuric acid manufacture is given by omitting some part for simplicity.]

1.   Draw the block diagram of this plant. For solution refer Fig. 7.9.

2.   Draw the process flow sheet of this plant. For solution refer Fig. 7.10.

Sol. :

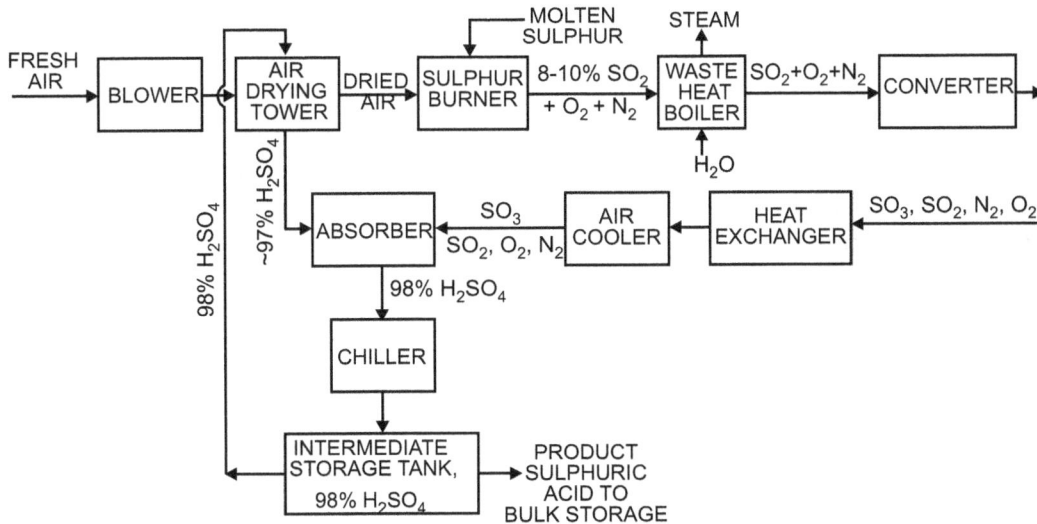

FIG. 7.9 : BLOCK DIAGRAM FOR PRODUCTION OF 98% SULPHURIC ACID

LEGEND / EQUIPMENT KEY

CODE	DESCRIPTION
B-1	BLOWER
ADT-1	AIR DRYING TOWER
BUN-1	BURNER
WHB-1	WASTE HEAT BOILER
R-1	REACTOR/CONVERTER
HE-1	HEAT EXCHANGER
AC-1	AIR COOLER
AB-1	ABSORBER
DCH-1	CHILLER-DOUBLE PIPE TYPE
IST-1	INTERMEDIATE STORAGE TANK

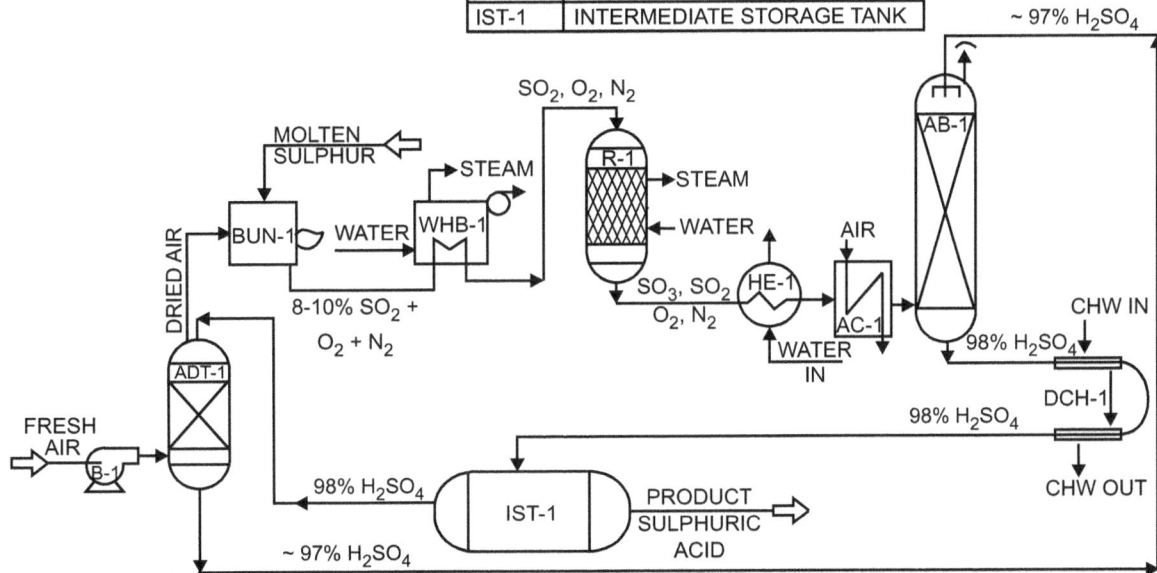

FIG. 7.10 : PROCESS FLOW SHEET FOR MANUFACTURE OF COMMERCIAL GRADE SULPHURIC ACID

Ex. 7.3 : Formaldehyde is produced by oxydehydrogenation of methanol. The air is heated in an air preheater and methanol is vaporised in a vaporiser. Then they are
mixed in the desired proportion and are introduced into a fixed bed reactor. The reactions occurring in the bed are :

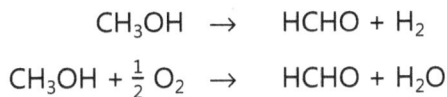

$$CH_3OH \rightarrow HCHO + H_2$$

$$CH_3OH + \tfrac{1}{2} O_2 \rightarrow HCHO + H_2O$$

The product gases containing formaldehyde, hydrogen, water, methanol, O_2 and N_2 are cooled in a heat exchanger using a suitable cooling medium. The exothermicity associated with the reactions is removed by passing compressed water on the shell side of the fixed bed reactor and utilised for producing low pressure steam. The cooled product gases are then introduced to a battery of scrubbers / absorbers in which formaldehyde and methanol are absorbed in water. The liquid mixture leaving the absorber containing formaldehyde, methanol and water is sent to an intermediate storage tank. The crude formaldehyde solution from the intermediate storage tank is then fed to a distillation column from the top of which methanol is obtained and is recycled to the vaporiser and formaldehyde in the form of formalin (37% formaldehyde solution) is removed as a bottom product. Draw the process flow diagram/sheet of this plant. Refer to Fig. 7.11.

Sol. :

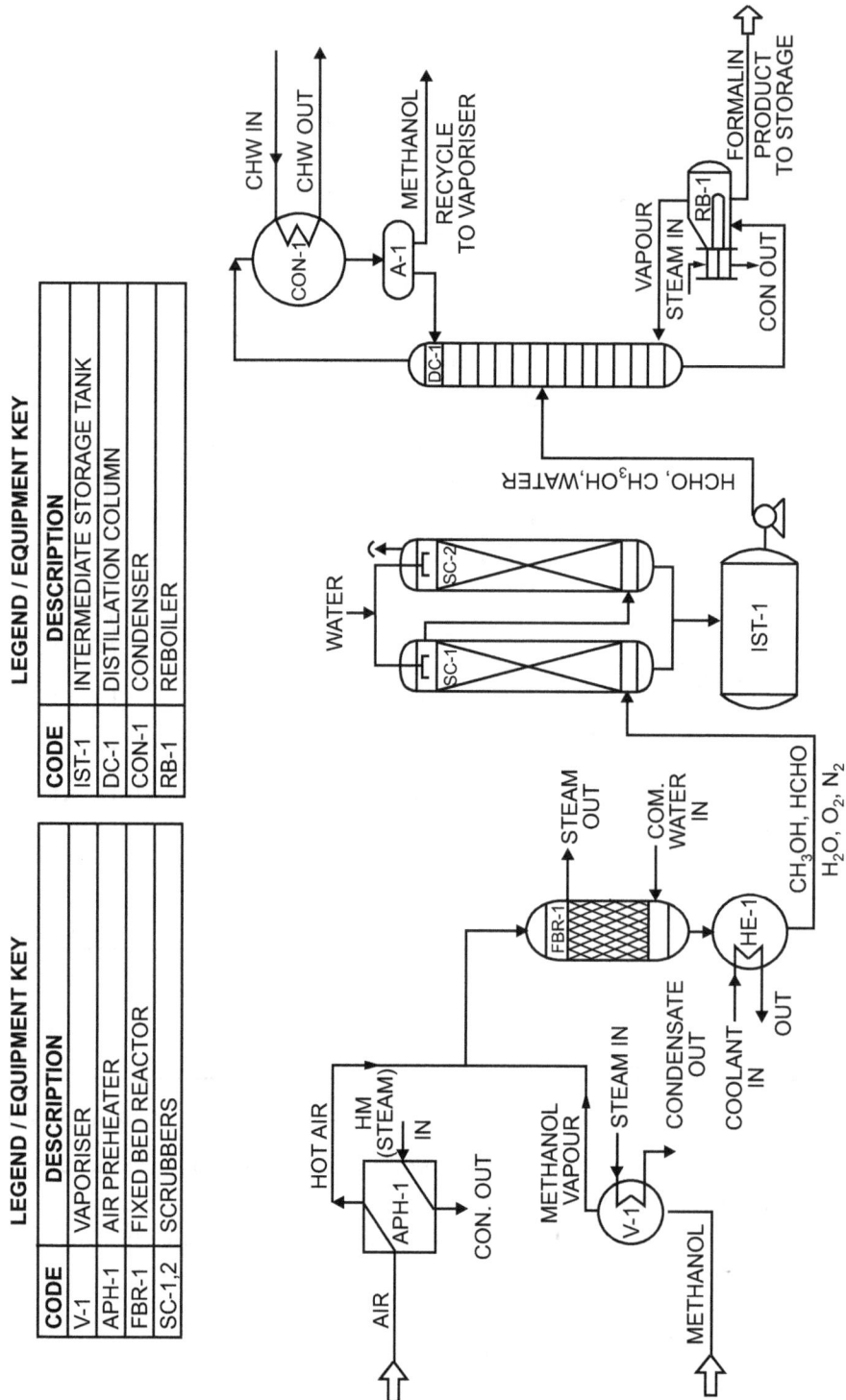

LEGEND / EQUIPMENT KEY

CODE	DESCRIPTION
V-1	VAPORISER
APH-1	AIR PREHEATER
FBR-1	FIXED BED REACTOR
SC-1,2	SCRUBBERS

LEGEND / EQUIPMENT KEY

CODE	DESCRIPTION
IST-1	INTERMEDIATE STORAGE TANK
DC-1	DISTILLATION COLUMN
CON-1	CONDENSER
RB-1	REBOILER

FIG. 7.11 : PROCESS FLOW SHEET FOR MANUFACTURE OF FORMALDEHYDE

Ex. 7.4 : Absolute alcohol is obtained by carrying out the fractional distillation of 96% by weight ethyl alcohol. The fresh feed (ethyl alcohol) is fed to an azeotropic column where benzene is used as an azeotrope breaker. The ternary azeotrope of ethanol, benzene and water is formed as the overhead which is condensed and phase separation is achieved in a decanter. From the decanter, the benzene rich layer is recycled to the azeotrope column (as reflux) and water rich layer is sent to a second fractionating column (a recovery column), where water is drained as bottoms. Almost ethanol + benzene is removed from the top of the recovery column which is recycled at the top of the azeotrope column. The bottom of the azeotrope column gives almost pure ethanol (99.5 %). Draw the process flow diagram/sheet for this plant. (Please see Fig. 7.12).

Sol. : Refer to Fig. 7.12.

Hint : A mixture of ethanol and water form an azeotrope at 96% by weight ethanol. For the separation of ethanol-water mixture we have to adopt a technique of azeotropic distillation using benzene as entrainer (azeotrope breaker). In the azeotropic distillation of this mixture, benzene is fed to the azeotropic column at the top and the feed is introduced centrally. It is assumed that the azeotropic column is a plate column while the recovery column is a packed column. For reboilers, steam is used as the heating medium and for condensers, chilled water is used as the cooling medium. 96% alcohol, absolute alcohol and benzene are all liquid at ambient temperature.

Ex. 7.5 : Ortho nitro aniline (ONA) is to be manufactured by ammination of ortho - nitro chlorobenzene (ONCB). Water is taken into a reactor (high pressure batch reactor) and ammonia (excess) is taken into it at a low temperature. Molten ONCB is then added to the reactor and mass in the reactor is heated with medium pressure steam, so as to reach reaction temperature and pressure. The reaction temperature is held constant over a period of eight hours for complete conversion of ONCB to ONA.

After the reaction is over, ammonia recovery is started. Ammonia from the reaction vessel is sparged into a mechanically agitated vessel via a pressure reducing valve. Ammonia is absorbed in water in the mechanically agitated vessel which is maintained at temperature less than 20°C by recirculating chilled water through a coil dipped in it.

The unabsorbed gas from the mechanically agitated vessel is sent to two scrubbers in series where it is further absorbed in water spread from the top of the scrubbers. Scrubbers are packed columns containing sadle packings. NH_3 liquor from the bottom of scrubber goes to a liquor storage tank which is kept in circulation till NH_3 recovery is complete. After recovery of ammonia, the product mass containing ONA is cooled to room temperature by cooling tower water, the product mass, i.e., slurry of ONA is then fed via a screw pump to a batch centrifuge. Wet ONA is then dried in a tray dryer and dried ONA is pulverised in a hammer mill to get product ONA in powder form. Reaction conditions are Temp = 169°C, Press = 41 kgf/cm^2.

Draw the process flow diagram of the above mentioned plant.

Sol. : Please see Fig. 7.13.

Hint : ONCB is a solid at ambient conditions (MP = 34°C). It is stored in a steam jacketed horizontal tank in molten form. A tracer line is provided from the storage tank to the reactor via measuring vessel to transfer ONCB from the tank to the reactor (not shown in the flow sheet). Shart drawing the process flow sheet by drawing an inflow arrow for the molten ONCB (thus avoiding storage and measuring vessels). The temperature of 20°C in the mechanically agitated vessel is maintained by using chilled water as a cooling medium. Medium pressure steam is to be used as a heating medium for the reactor.

Ex. 7.6 : Separation of n - Butanol - water is carried out in a two step process. The process starts by charging the original mixture (fresh feed) to a decanter which operates at a temperature below the boiling point. The butanol - rich phase from the decanter is fed to a stripping column (plate column). This column produces high purity alcohol as the bottom product and an overhead vapour which approaches the azeotropic composition. The aqueous phase from the stripping column is fed to a second stripper which produces butanol free water as a bottom product. Since water is the bottom product from this column, open steam can be used to provide reboil vapour. The aqueous column also produces a top vapour which approaches the azeotropic composition. Overhead vapour streams from both columns are condensed in a common condenser and then fed to the decanter along with the fresh feed. Draw the process flow diagram / sheet of this plant.

The stripping column and striper are both plate columns and named as mentioned as they form the stripping section of a fractionating column. Butanol forms an azeotrope with water.

Sol. : Refer to Fig. 7.14.

Ex. 7.7 : Acetone is produced by catalytic dehydrogenation of isopropyl alcohol. Isopropyl alcohol is vaporized, heated and fed to a catalytic reactor (fixed bed reactor), where it undergoes catalytic dehydrogenation to acetone. The reactor exist gases (acetone, hydrogen and unreacted isopropyl alcohol) pass to a condenser where most of the acetone, water and alcohol condense out. The final traces of acetone and alcohol are removed in a water scrubber. The effluent from the scrubber is combined with the condensate from the condenser, and distilled in a column to produce pure acetone and an effluent consisting of the water and alcohol. This effluent is distilled in a second column to separate the excess water. The product (distillate) from the second column is an azeotrope of water and isopropyl alcohol containing approximately 11 percent alcohol. It is recycled to the reactor. Zinc oxide or copper is used as the catalyst, and the reaction is carried out at a temperature of 400 to 500°C and 40 to 50 psig pressure. Draw the process flow diagram of this plant.

Sol. : Refer to Fig. 7.15.

LEGEND / EQUIPMENT KEY

NO.	CODE	DESCRIPTION
1	ADC-1	AZEOTROPIC DISTILLATION COLUMN
2	RC-1	RECOVERY COLUMN
3	C-1, C-2	CONDENSERS
4	RB-1,2	REBOILERS (THERMOSYPHON) TYPE
5	D-1	DECANTER
6	AC-1	ACCUMULATOR

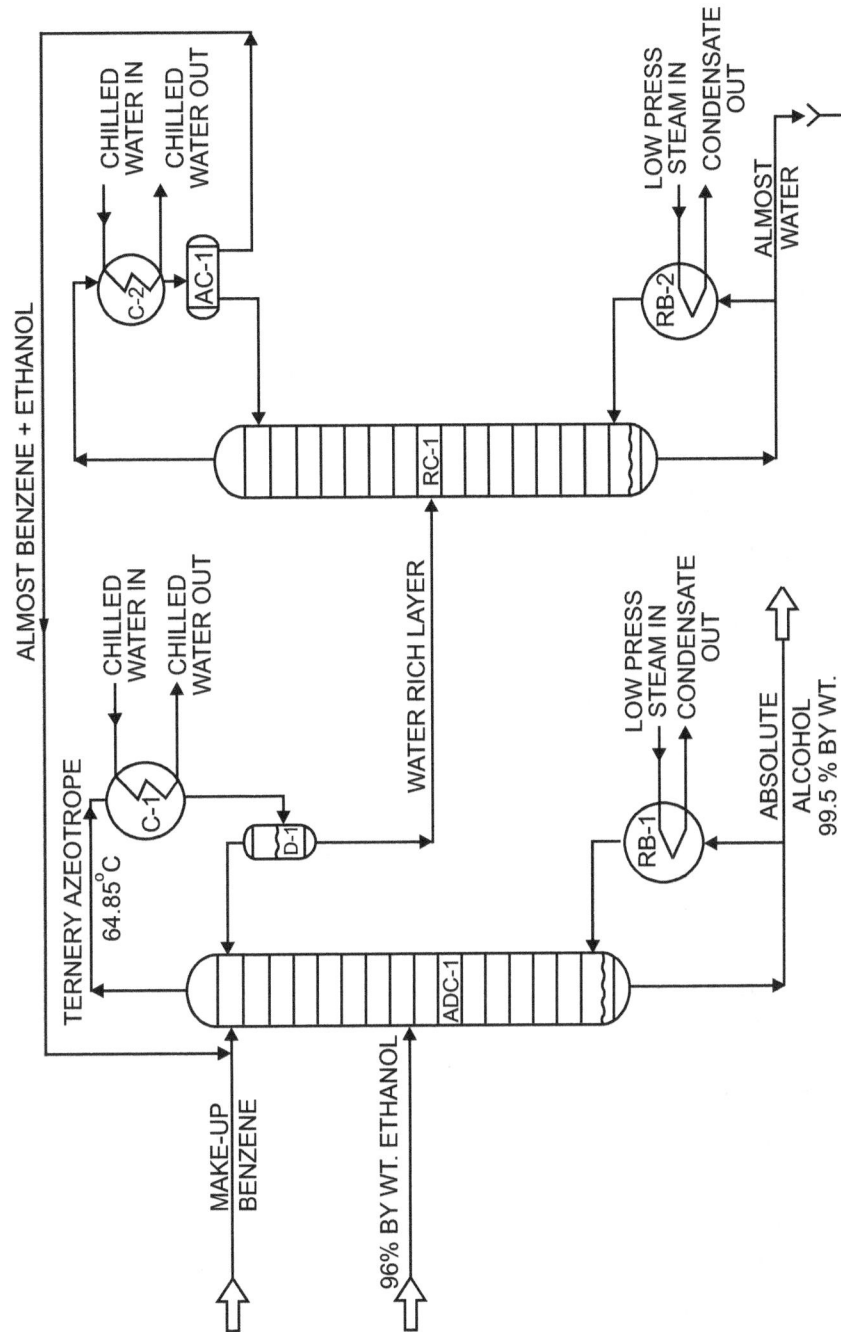

CHILLED WATER IN

CHILLED WATER OUT

C-2

AC-1

LOW PRESS STEAM IN

CONDENSATE OUT

RB-2

ALMOST WATER

ALMOST BENZENE + ETHANOL

RC-1

WATER RICH LAYER

CHILLED WATER IN

CHILLED WATER OUT

C-1

D-1

TERNERY AZEOTROPE 64.85°C

LOW PRESS STEAM IN

CONDENSATE OUT

RB-1

ABSOLUTE ALCOHOL 99.5 % BY WT.

ADC-1

MAKE-UP BENZENE

96% BY WT. ETHANOL

FIG. 7.12 : PROCESS FLOW SHEET OF DEHYDRATION OF 96% ETHANOL TO ABSOLUTE ALCOHOL BY AZEOTROPIC DISTILLATION USING BENZENE AS A ENTRAINER

LEGEND / EQUIPMENT KEY

NO.	CODE	DESCRIPTION
1	BR-1	BATCH REACTOR
2	MAV-1	MECHANICALLY AGITATED VESSEL
3	SC-1,2	SCRUBBERS
4	C-1	CENTRIFUGE (BASKET)

LEGEND / EQUIPMENT KEY

NO.	CODE	DESCRIPTION
5	TD-1	TRAY DRYER
6	HM-1	HAMMER MILL
7	ST-1	NH$_3$ LIQUOR STORAGE TANK
8	P-1,2	TRANSFER PUMPS

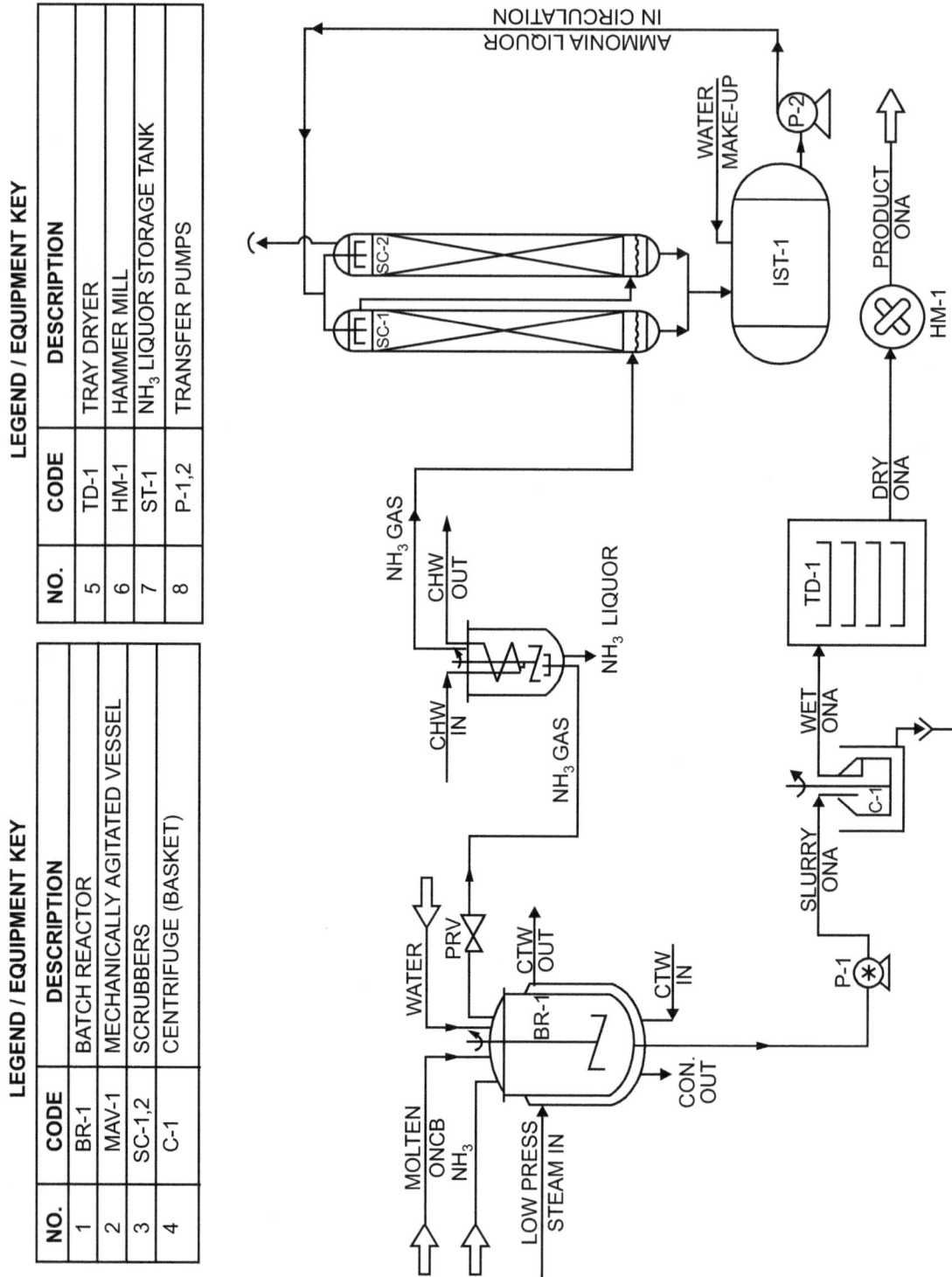

FIG. : 7.13 : PROCESS FLOW SHEET DIAGRAM – MANUFACTURE OF ONA BY AMMONOLYSIS OF ONCB

LEGEND / EQUIPMENT KEY

NO.	CODE	DESCRIPTION
1	BC-1	BUTANOL COLUMN (STRIPPING COLUMN)
2	AC-2	AQUEOUS COLUMN
3	D-1	DECANTER
4	CON-1	CONDENSER
5	RB-1	REBOILER

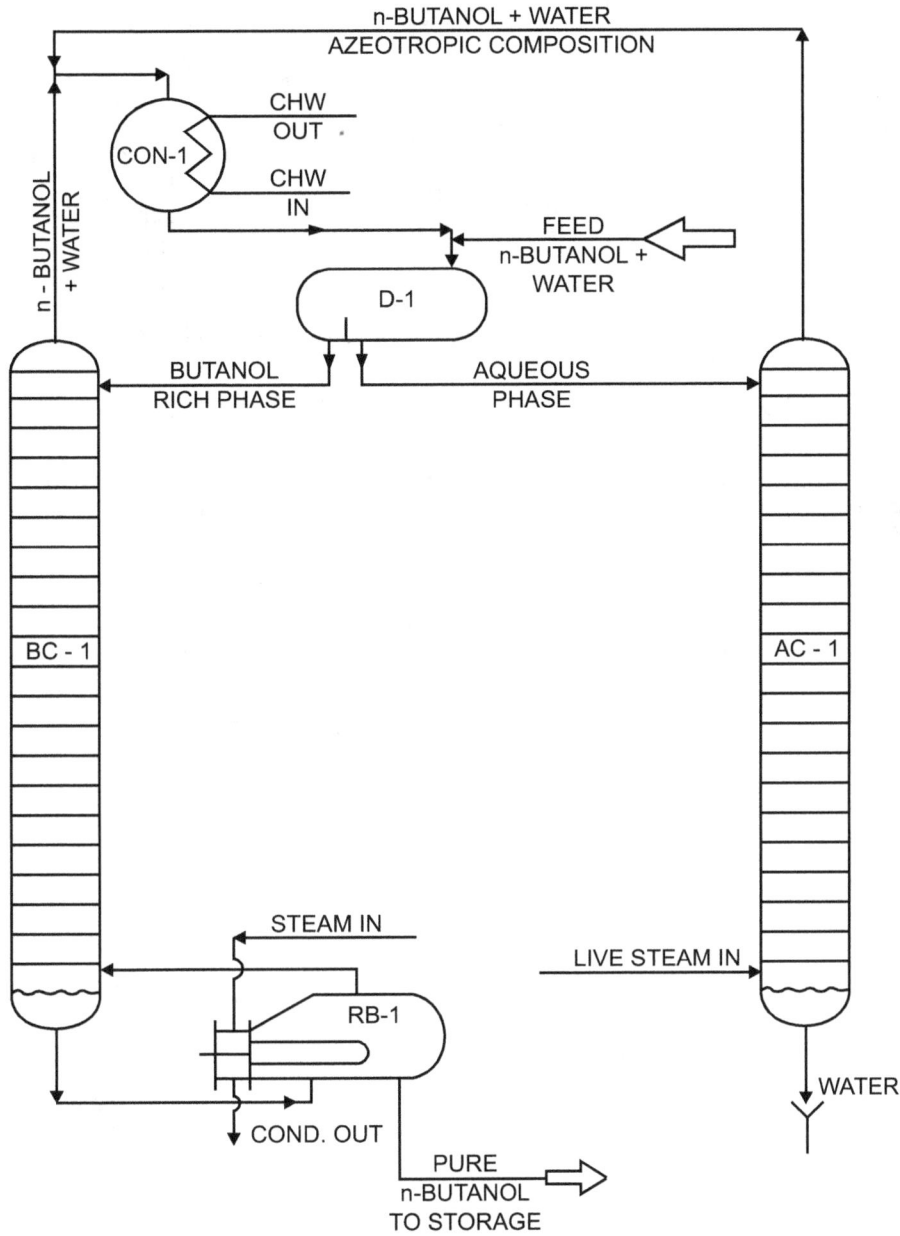

n-BUTANOL + WATER
AZEOTROPIC COMPOSITION

CON-1

CHW OUT

CHW IN

FEED
n-BUTANOL + WATER

n - BUTANOL + WATER

D-1

BUTANOL RICH PHASE

AQUEOUS PHASE

BC - 1

AC - 1

STEAM IN

LIVE STEAM IN

RB-1

COND. OUT

PURE
n-BUTANOL
TO STORAGE

WATER

FIG. 7.14 : PROCESS FLOW SHEET SEPARATION OF N - BUTANOL AND WATER BY TWO - COLUMN SYSTEM

LEGEND / EQUIPMENT KEY

CODE	DESCRIPTION
V-1	VAPORISER
PH-1	PREHEATER
R-1	CATALYTIC REACTOR
C-1,2,3	CONDENSERS
CL-1,2	DISTILLATION COLUMNS
RB-1,2	REBOILERS
SC-1	SCRUBBER
A-1,2	ACCUMULATORS
CHW	CHILLED WATER

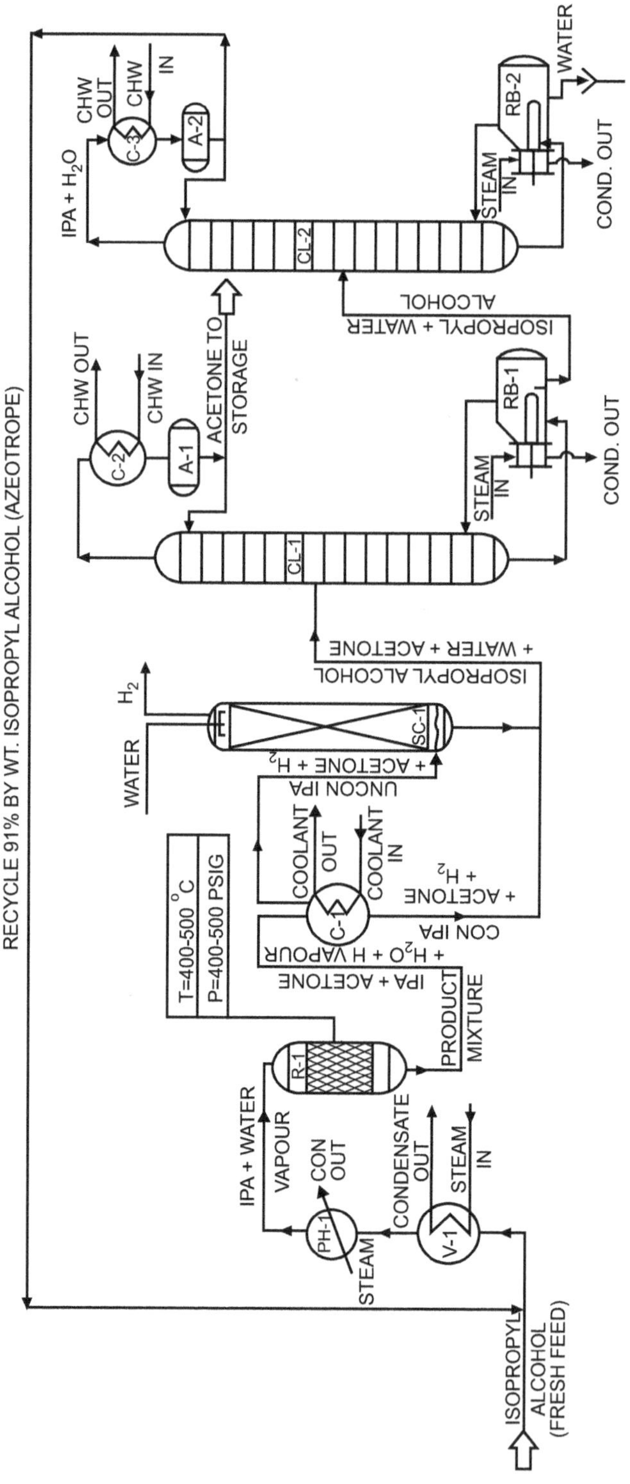

FIG. 7.15 : PROCESS FLOW SHEET - MANUFACTURE OF ACETONE BY DEHYDROGENATION OF ISOPROPYL ALCOHOL

7.1.3 Utility Flow Sheet (Utility Line Diagram)

Utility line diagrams cover the utilities (auxiliary services) required such as electricity, steam, water (cooling tower water/chilled water), air, etc.

The utilities like electricity, steam, water, etc. are required for most of the chemical plants. These utilities do not participate in an actual process but are essential to carry out the process-without which we cannot convert the raw materials into finished products. Various utilities are used in industry as per need.

The utilities used in the chemical industry include electricity, steam (low pressure, medium pressure), hot water, heating oils such as marlotherm and therminol, heat transfer mediums such as dowtherm, cooling tower water, chilled water, air, refrigerants (e.g., ammonia).

This diagram gives us idea regarding the various utilities required for carrying out a particular operation or a step involved in the manufacturing process.

A pipe line (of large diameter) carrying a certain utility from the utility generating unit into the process plant from which branched lines (tappings) are given to various equipments as per need/requirement is called a header line, header or service header, e.g., low pressure steam header. The utility in the plant after its use in a certain operation is returned to the utility generating unit (exceptions - air, electricity) due to economic consideration through a pipe line to which branched lines from various equipment for returning it. This pipe line is called a return header (e.g., cooling tower water return header, condensate header - a return header for steam). The branched lines or tappings are to be shown as full dots on a line representing the header. The headers are usually led at the level of first floor (i.e., at an elevation of 4 to 5 m). When ULD is drawn floorwise separately or when coupled with ELD (Engineering line diagram), the headers are usually shown beneath the first floor.

A utility line diagram (ULD) is basically a process flow sheet along with headers (incoming and return headers), branched lines or tappings from the headers to process equipments (and from the process equipments to headers) and valves for the process and utility lines.

The simplest method of drawing the utility line diagram (ULD) is (i) draw the headers required (incoming and return headers) at the top of the drawing sheet (for each utility draw first the incoming header and then draw the return header below it with a gap of 4 to
5 mm between them), (ii) draw the process flow sheet below the headers drawn, (iii) draw branched lines - utility connections from incoming headers to process equipments and from the equipments to the return headers as per requirement (i.e., based upon the requirement of utility or utilities for the operations involved in the process) and (iv) draw the appropriate valves required for the process and utility/service lines. [OR (i) draw the incoming headers at the top of the drawing sheet, (ii) draw the process flow sheet below the incoming headers and (iii) draw the return headers below the process flow sheet and do the branched conections].

For utility headers and branched lines/tappings, the service fluid codes piping given in IS-9446-1980 must be used.

Before drawing a ULD of a given process, we have to find out the utility or utilities needed for carrying out each step involved in the process based on the process description.

When a utility line diagram (ULD) is to be drawn separately and without taking into consideration the elevations of process equipments and header lines then the utility/utilities needed for a particular step/operation involved in the process are shown on the ULD as follows :

Example

Assume that the given process involves a batch reactor in which certain reaction is to be carried out. The batch reactor needs low pressure steam for heating and cooling tower water for cooling the reaction mass.

The utility line diagram for this particular step is shown in Fig. 7.16. Here the process lines are intentionally omitted. The utility headers are drawn with a distance of 5 to 6 mm between them. The return header for a particular utility should be drawn immediately after the main header.

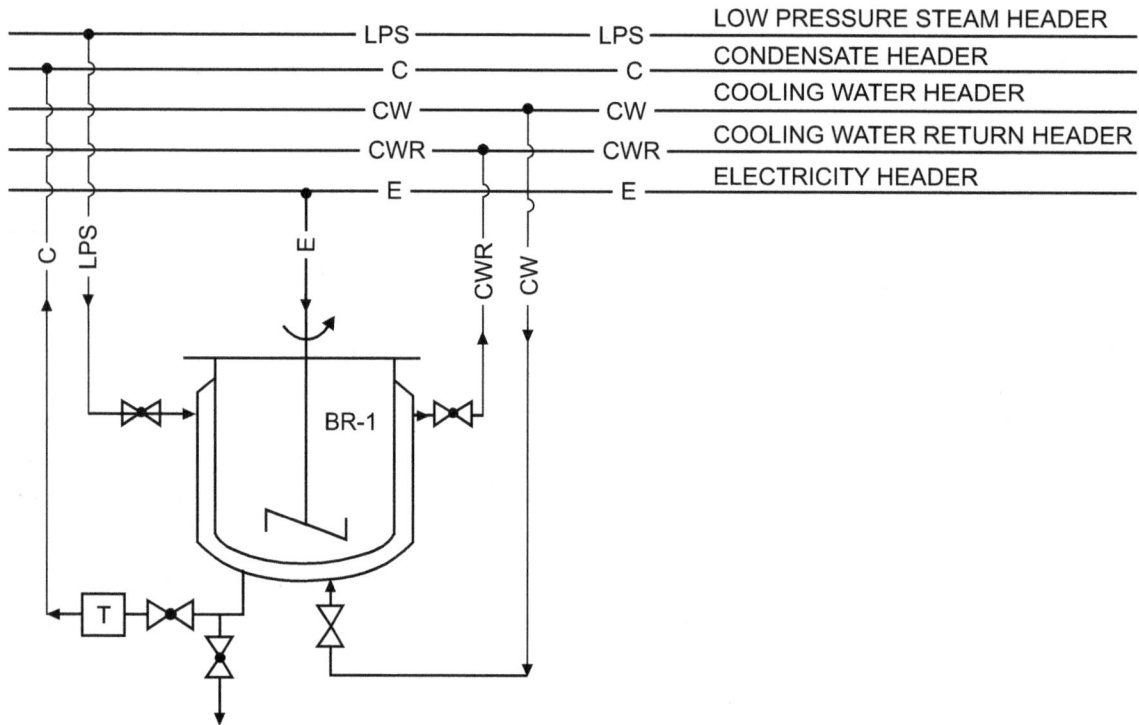

Fig. 7.16 (A) : ULD for batch reactor (Drawn without indicating process lines)

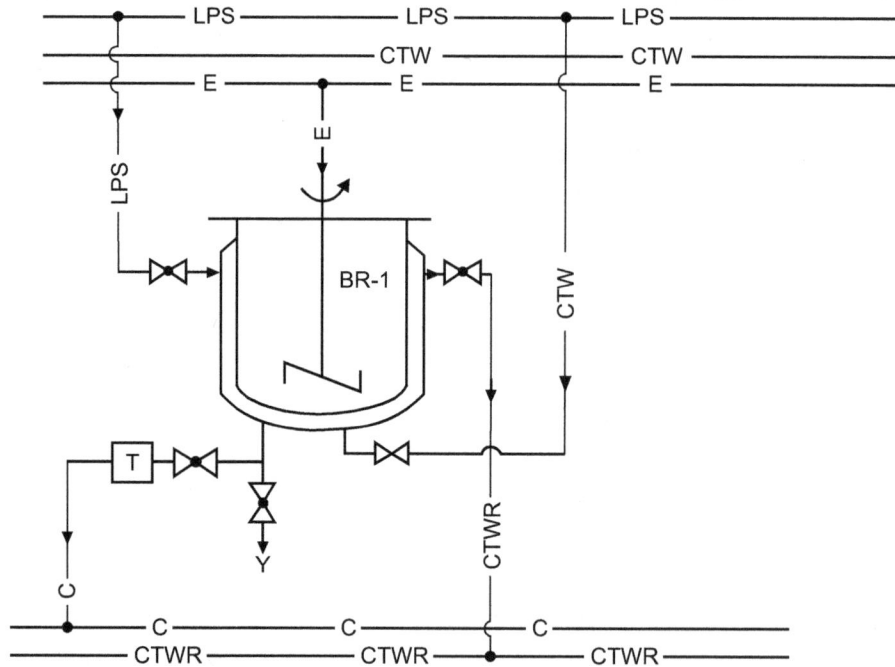

Fig. 7.16 (B) : Alternate form of ULD for batch reactor (Drawn without showing process lines)

Sometimes to show utilities needed for a particular operation, it becomes necessary to do some additions in the process flow sheet symbol drawn, e.g., assume that a particular process involves a tray dryer for drying of wet solids then in this case we have to show a fan as well as a heating coil to show the required utilities. [Refer Fig. 7.17]

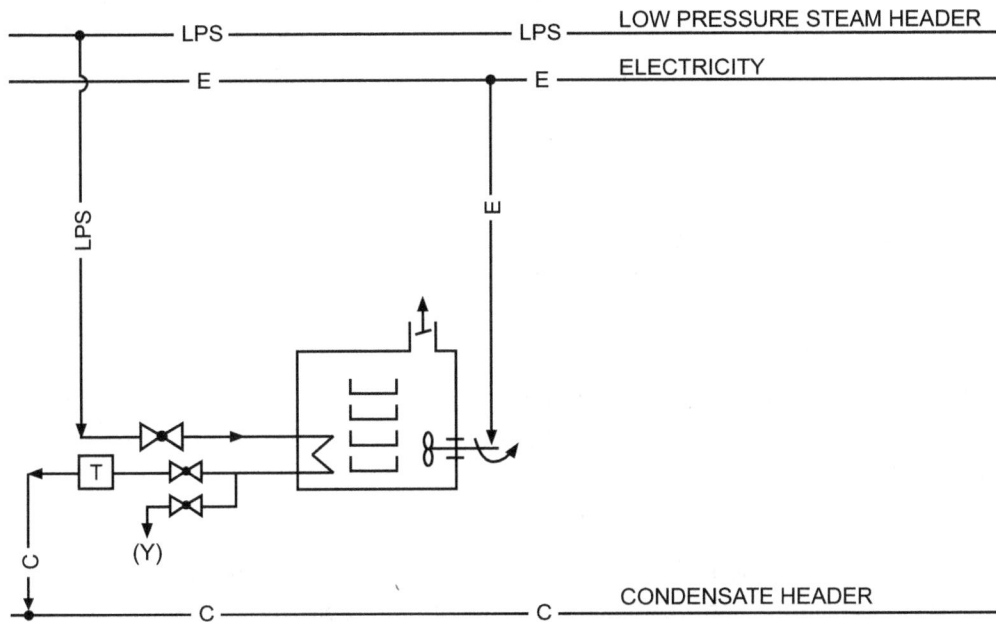

Fig. 7.17 : ULD for tray dryer (without process lines)

UTILITY BLOCK DIAGRAM (UBD)

The utilities like electricity, steam, water, etc. are required by most of the chemical process plants. These utilities are located at a certain distance from the processing area and storage of a chemical plant.

The utility block diagram can be drawn separately for each utility or it can be coupled with a lay-out of the ground floor of the processing area, where all the required utility generating units are represented by rectangular blocks (for electricity - show electrical main panel board, for steam-show boiler house, for air-show compressor house, for cooling water-show cooling tower, for chilled water/refrigerant-show refrigeration plant and for hot oil show furnace as a utility generating unit).

To draw utility block diagram separately for each utility, draw rectangular blocks for the utility generating unit and the process equipments needing that utility.

Fig. 7.18 shows a utility block diagram for steam. Here it is assumed that the process equipments - reactor, heater and reboilers all require low pressure steam as a utility.

ELECTRICITY

Electricity is a very important and useful form of power for the chemical industries. Careful consideration must be given to the source, cost and reliability of the primary electric power supply. Power can be either purchased from a public or private utility, produced at the plant site by steam driven turbogenerators or natural gas driven engines or purchased from an adjacent industrial plant. There are many factors which govern the design, installation, and maintenance of industrial plant power systems. The major electrical design items include power generation or purchased power substation and switching, distribution systems, power wiring for plant equipment, lighting equipment, safety equipment, electrical process control systems, etc.

Starting at the source of power supply, basic electrical system includes main transformer, switch board with OCB and main panel board in the electric yard. The individual equipments are separately fed through feeder wires from the main panel board as per their requirement. Based on KVA rating, dimensions of transformer are fixed which in turn fix the dimensions of a transformer yard. The transformer can be located inside the building or kept open to the sky. Depending upon the power requirement including lighting equipment, etc. the dimensions of OCB room and main panel board are fixed.

STEAM

Steam is generated in boilers by burning either a solid fuel such as coal, bagasse or a liquid fuel such as furnace oil, light diesel oil. An adequate provision must be made for storage of solid or liquid fuel. Based upon the type of boiler and its size (capacity), the boiler space requirement in the form of a building is fixed. Feed water to boilers is usually demineralised soft water. Depending upon the requirement of such a water, the space required for a soft and demineralised water plant is fixed.

WATER

Cooling water (which is soft) used in the process industry is kept in circulation. The make up water is to be provided to cooling towers. Based upon the cooling water requirement, the size of cooling tower(s) and soft water plant is fixed which in turn fixes the space requirement of cooling tower(s). Cooling towers are located at free space so as to have fresh air available easily.

Chilled water/chilled brine is produced by installing the refrigeration unit /plant of required capacity. The capacity of refrigeration unit specified in terms of tonnes of refrigeration. These units are always located inside the building nearby the processing area.

AIR

In industry, compressed air is required for many purposes. It is obtained with the help of a compressor. Particularly big and complex plants are controlled by automatic controllers. These controllers are invariably pneumatically operated. Refineries and petrochemical plants must use pneumatic controllers. Based on the requirement of compressed air, instrument air etc. and pressure, the type and size of compressor and auxiliary units for removal of oil, grease, moisture etc. is fixed which in turn fixes the space requirement of a compressor house.

The utilities such as electricity, steam, water, air etc. are usually arranged in one row away from the main plant and the space requirement is obtained from actual suppliers of these units. UBD may be drawn separately for each individual utility or can be coupled with the layout of a processing area or plot plan.

Following example will give idea regarding drawing of UBD for utility such as steam. Assume that a process involves process equipments such as reactor, heater and two reboilers which require low pressure steam as utility.

STEAM HEADER

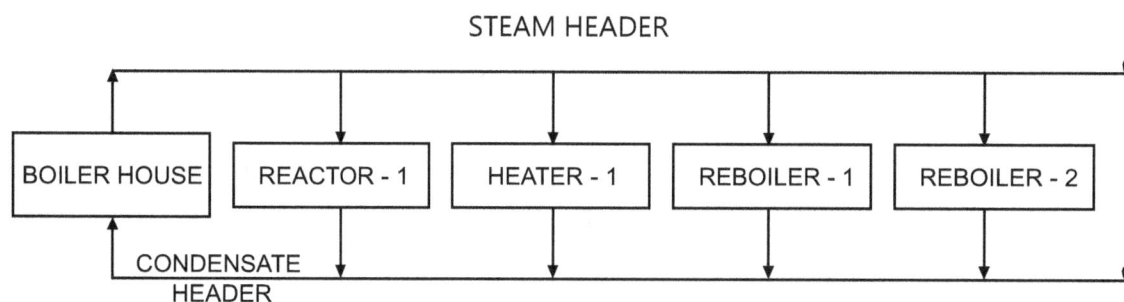

Fig. 7.18 : UBD for steam

Ex. 7.8 : Draw the utility line diagram for the process of manufacture of orthonitroaniline given in Ex. 7.6.

Sol. : The utilities to be used are : (i) medium pressure steam for the reactor and dryer, (ii) cooling tower water to the reactor, (iii) chilled water to the mechanically agitated vessel and (iv) electricity for the reactor, mechanically agitated vessel, centrifuge, dryer (for its fan) and the transfer pumps. Globe valve is used for the steam line, globe valve and steam trap to the condensate line. Gate at the inlet of cooling tower water and globle at the exit of it for the reactor. Plug valves are used for chilled water. Please see Fig. 7.19.

Ex. 7.9 : Draw the utility line diagram for process of azeotropic distillation for production of absolute alcohol given in Ex. 7.4.

Sol. : Refer to Fig. 7.20.

VALVE	NAME
—▷◁—	BUTTERFLY
—▷◁—	GATE
—▷◁—	GLOBE
—▷◁—	BALL
—▷◁—	PLUG

LEGEND / EQUIPMENT KEY

CODE	DESCRIPTION
BR-1	BATCH REACTOR
MAV-1	MECHANICAL AGITATED VESSEL
SC-1,2	SCRUBBERS
ST-1	STORAGE TANK
HM-1	HAMMER MILL
TD-1	TRAY DRIER
C-1	CENTRIFUGE
PRV	PRESSURE REDUCING VALVE
P-1	SCREW PUMP
P-2	CENTRIFUGAL PUMP

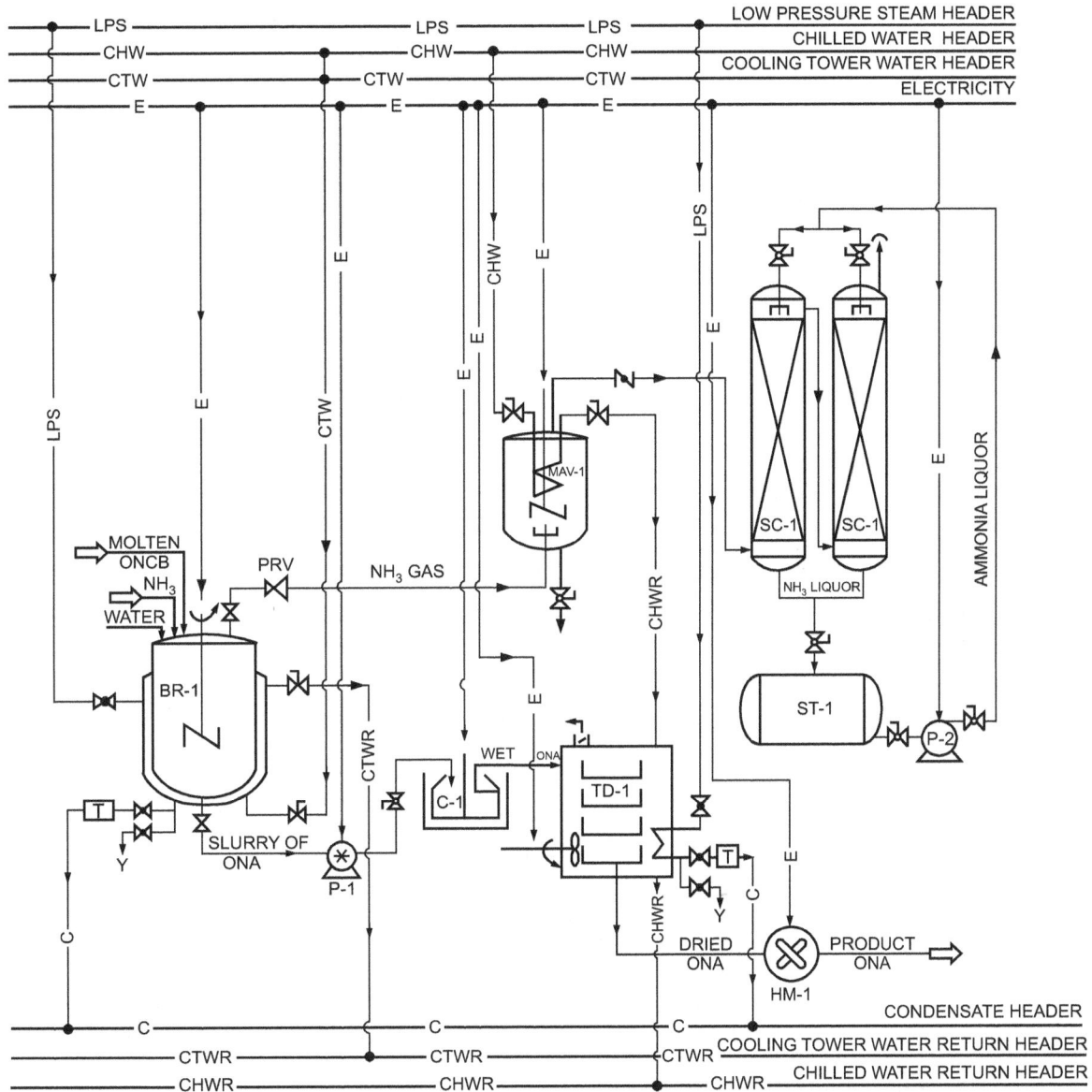

FIG. 7.19 : UTILITY LINE DIAGRAM - MANUFACTURE OF ONA BY AMMONOLYSIS OF ONCB

LEGEND / EQUIPMENT KEY

CODE	DESCRIPTION	CODE	DESCRIPTION
ADC-1	AZEOTROPIC DISTILLATION COLUMN	RB-1,2	REBOILERS
RC-1	RECOVERY COLUMN	D-1	DECANTER
C-1,2	CONDENSERS	AC-1	ACCUMULATOR

SYMBOL	VALVE
—▷◁—	GLOBE
—▷◁—	BALL
—N—	BUTTERFLY

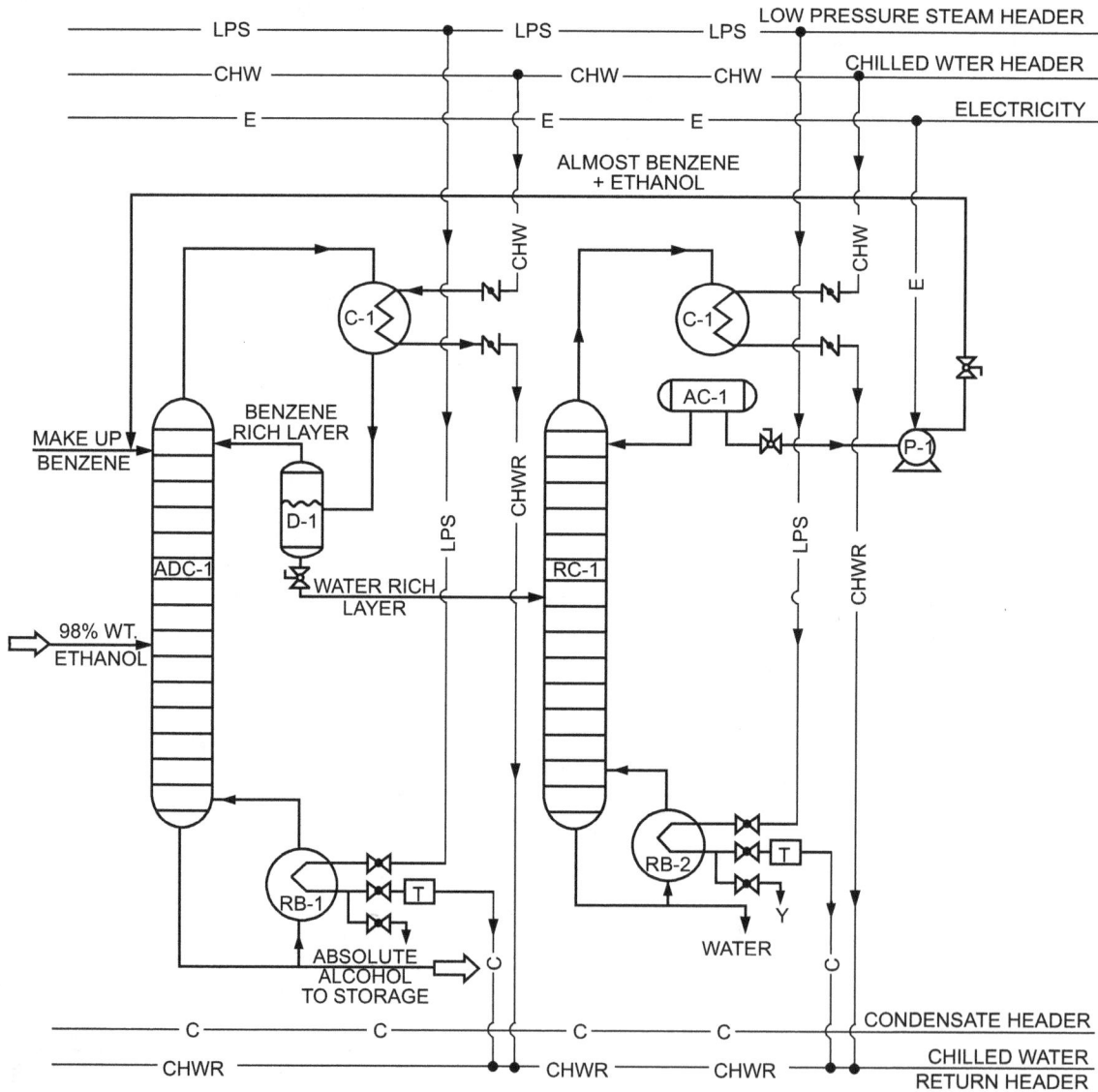

FIG. 7.20 : UTILITY LINE DIAGRAM FOR PRODUCTION OF ABSOLUTE ALCOHOL BY AZEOTROPIC DISTILLATION OF 96% BY WT. ETHANOL USING BENZENE AS A ENTRAINER

Ex. 7.10 : Draw the utility block diagram for the utilities such as steam and chilled water required for the plant described in Ex. 7.5.

Sol. : Refer to Fig. 7.21.

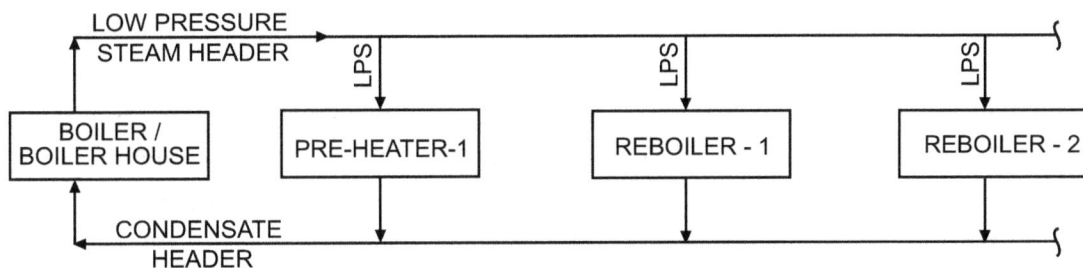

FIG. 7.21 (A) : UTILITY BLOCK DIAGRAM FOR STEAM

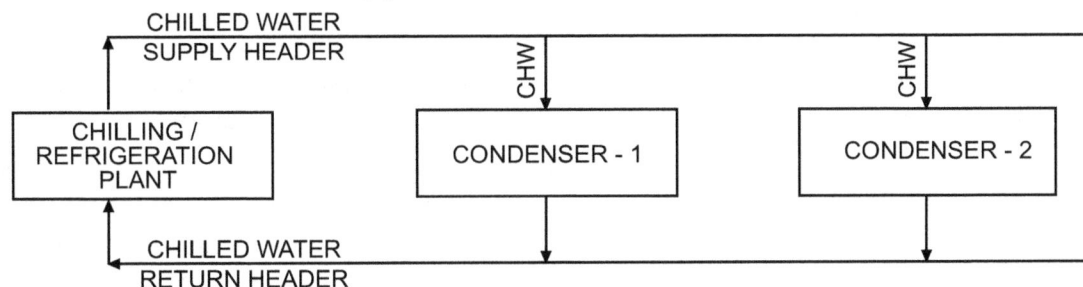

FIG. 7.21 (B) : UTILITY BLOCK DIAGRAM FOR CHILLED WATER

7.2 PIPING AND INSTRUMENTATION DIAGRAM

The Piping and Instrumentation diagram (P and I diagram) is based on the process flow sheet and shows the engineering details of the equipments, instruments and controls, piping, pumps, valves and fittings, along with their arrangement. This diagam is also called the Engineering Flow-sheet or Mechanical Flow-sheet or Engineering Line Diagram (LED). P and I diagrams are of fundamental importance in all phases of the life of the plant.

A P and I diagram should include :

(i)　All process equipments, with each equipment identified by an equipment code and number. Each equipment should be drawn in proportion and all nozzle connections should be shown.

(ii)　All pipes, identified by a line identification number. The diameter of the pipe, its material of construction and insulation requirement should be included as part of the line identification number (for each line).

(iii)　Direction of flow.

(iv)　Key dimensions of all equipments.

(v)　Equipment elevations.

(vi)　All valves including control valves along with an identification number, type and size. The type of valve is shown by the symbol used for the valve. Symbols for valves are given in the Indian Standard IS-9446-1980 and the same should be used.

(vii)　All control loops and instruments with an identification number and standard symbols for controllers and instruments are given in the Indian Standard IS-9446-1980. We have to use them.

(viii)　Transportation devices, identified by a suitable identification number. The type is shown by the symbol used for the transportion device. Use symbols as per IS-3232.

(ix)　All operations and stream conditions. Operating and design pressures and temperatures for all process equipments and reactors.

(x)　Auxiliary services/utilities required.

(xi)　Drainage requirements, all pipe-line drains, by-passes and vents.

If the process is simple and involves only a few steps, then the utility lines (headers and tappings) can be shown on the P and I diagram. For complex processes, only the utility/service connections (to show the utilities required) should be shown on the P and I diagram and we are adopting this practice in drawing P and I diagrams (i.e. we will be showing utilities by arrows-indicating the utility/service connections).

(i)　　The P and I diagram should be drawn floor-wise. The floor to floor distance to be taken (while drawing this diagram) may range from 5 to 9 metres.

(ii)　　The P and I diagram should be drawn to scale if the overall dimensions of the equipments are provided. When the dimensions are not provided then the equipments are to be drawn proportionately.

(iii)　　The P and I diagram gives us idea regarding the elevation of a plant (vertical dimensions of a plant) and floor-wise installation/placing of the equipments. We can very easily draw a layout of the processing area, i.e., an equipment layout by referring to this diagram. The P and I diagram serves as the basis to draw a layout of equipments.

(iv)　　In this diagram, simple schematic elevation views of the equipments (diagrammatic sketch resembling to the equipments as closest as possible) involving in a process are used instead of their flow-sheet symbols and these can be altered in such a way that all connections will appear on the plane of the diagram.

(v)　　If there is no special reason for elevating equipments, it should be located on the ground floor. Some equipments are elevated, i.e., placed on floors other than the ground floor for specific reasons - (i) to simplify the plant operations (feeding of reactors from elevated tanks to take the advantage of gravity flow), (ii) to enable the system to operate (holding tanks are elevated high enough to provide an adequate NPSH for the pump below) and (iii) for plant safety.

Heavy duty machines such as compressors, centrifuges and size reduction machines-pulverisers are usually located on the ground floor to maximum on the first floor to avoid vibrations of the total factory building. The drying of materials is often the final operation in a manufacturing process and the product from a dryer is often ready for final packaging. Therefore, dryers are usually located on the ground floor. Crystallisers may be located on the first floor to feed slurry from them to the centrifuges placed below - on the ground floor-to take the advantage of gravity flow. Reboilers are generally placed on the ground floor and distillation columns are elevated high enough from the ground floor, so vapours from a reboiler are fed directly at the bottom of the adjoining column. Pumps are generally located on the ground floor but they can be located on floors other than the ground floor depending upon process requirements.

(vi)　　Equipments are supported by supports. Horizontal process equipments are supported by saddle supports and vertical equipments are supported by bracket or skirt supports. Therefore, in the P and I diagram of any process, each process equipment need to be elevated to a certain height (at least 1 m) from the floor on which it is placed or installed whenever it is possible to show the type of support used then it should be shown in the diagram.

In the P & I diagram, fluid moving machineries such as pumps, blowers etc., or solid handling devices are shown by their respective flow sheet symbols as per IS-3232 (i.e., flow sheet symbols are retained for the transportation devices).

For example :

Pump on
ground floor

Fig. 7.22

In the P and I diagram, a batch reactor located on the ground floor – elevated at a certain distance from the floor (with bracket support) will appear as :

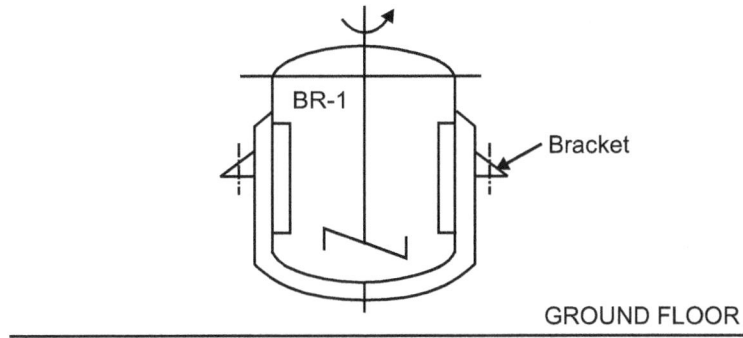

Fig. 7.23

A stir tank crystalliser (cooling type) embedded in the first floor and a basket centrifuge located on the ground floor will appear in the P & I diagram as :

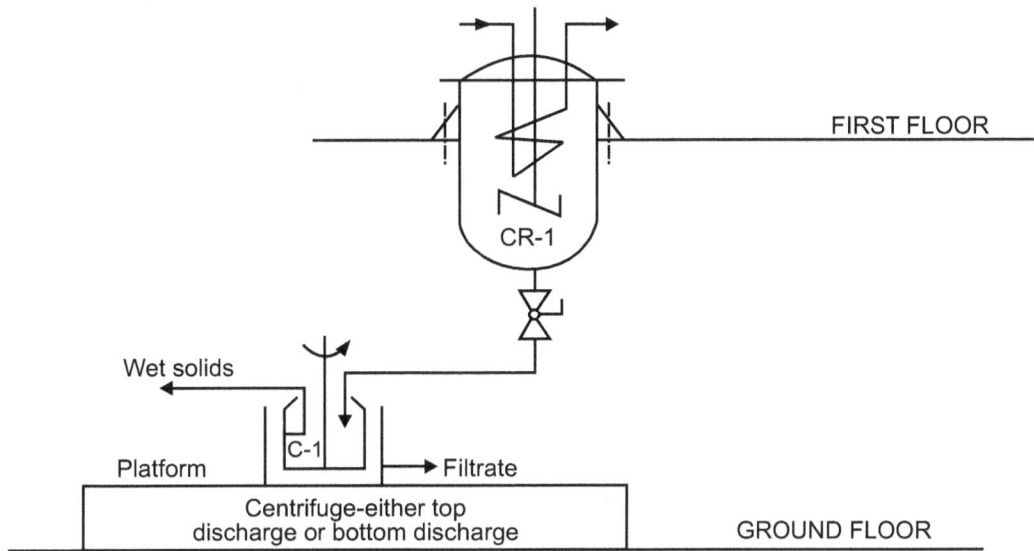

Fig. 7.24

An absorption column (packed column) located on the ground floor extending above the first floor will appear as :

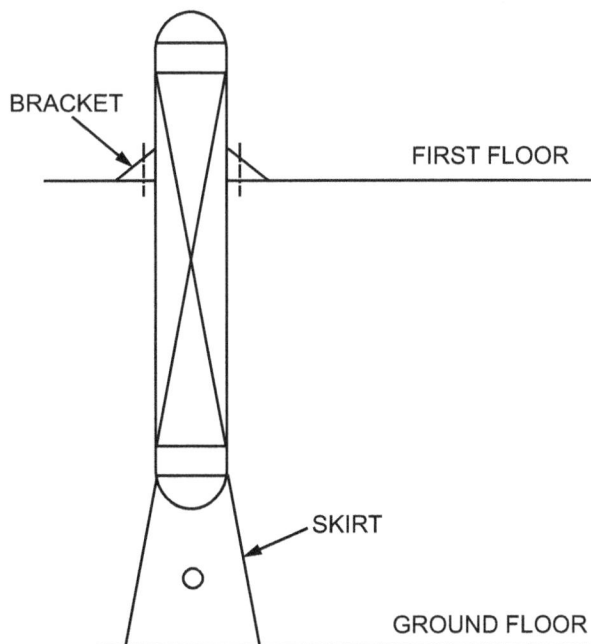

Fig. 7.25

In the P & I diagram, we have to use simple schematic elevation views of the process equipments involved instead of their flow sheet symbols. Fig. 7.26 shows simple elevation views of some process equipments to be used in P & I diagrams.

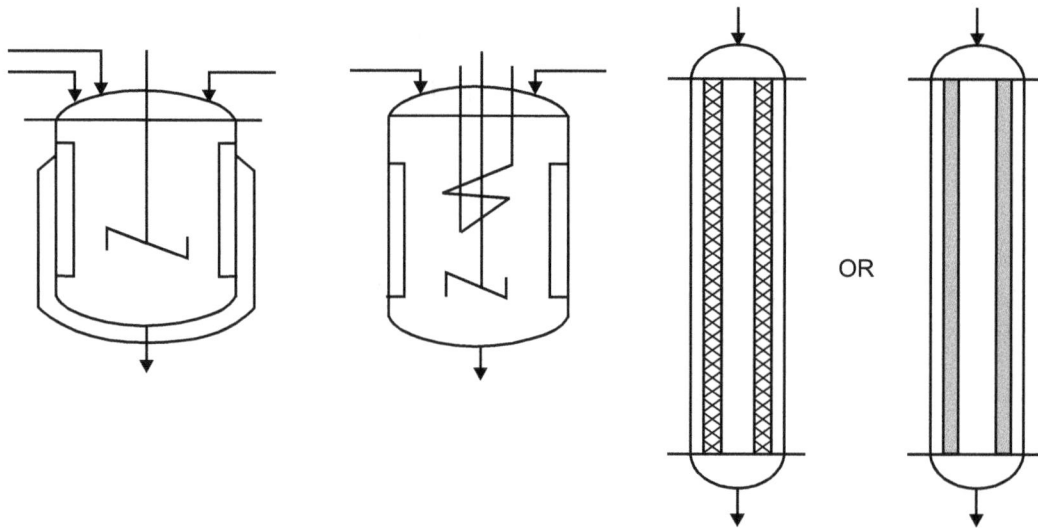

Batch reactor / Semi batch reactor / Jacketed vessel   **Mechanically agitated vessel**   **Fixed bed reactor**

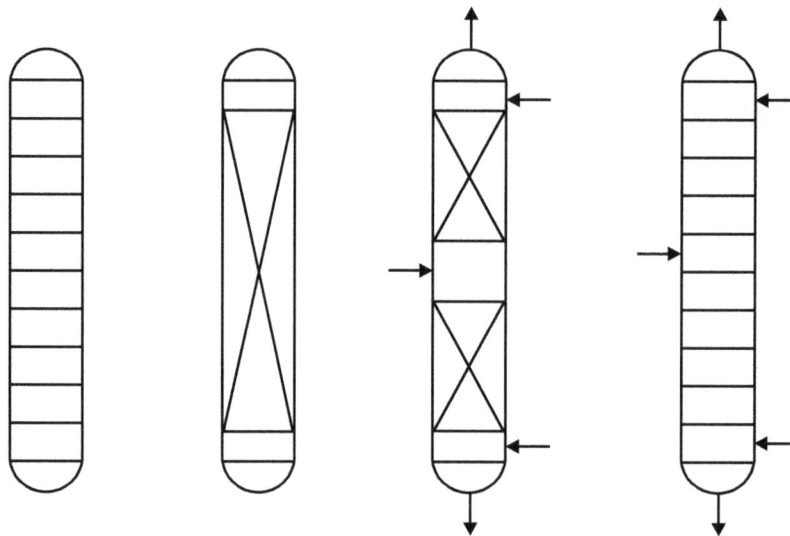

Plate and packed columns used for mass transfer

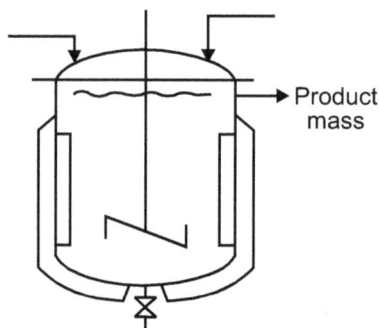

Jacketed CSTR

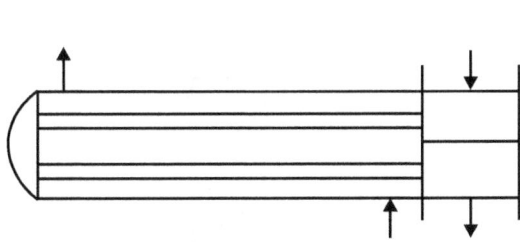

Heat exchanger / Cooler / Condenser

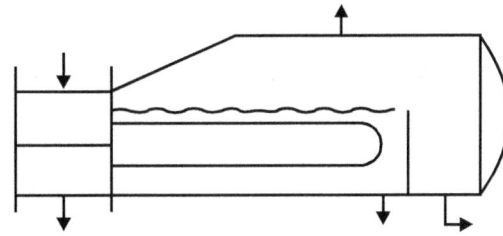

Kettle reboiler

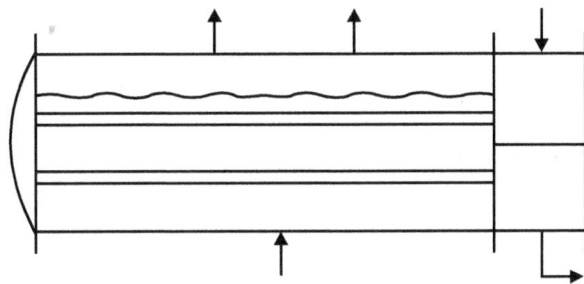

Vaporiser / horizontal thermosyphon reboiler

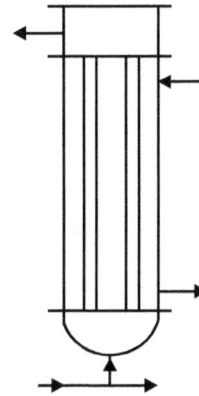

Vertical thermosyphon reboiler

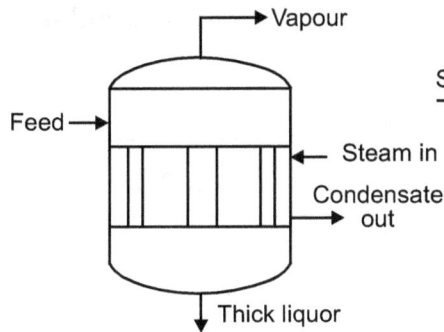

Short tube vertical evaporator

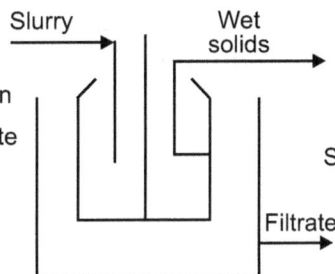

Batch centrifuge

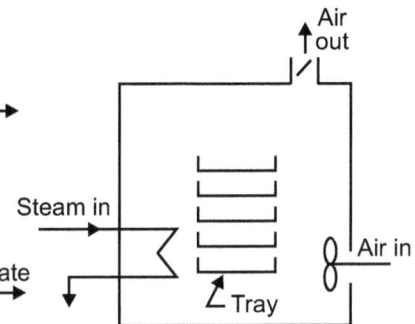

Tray dryer

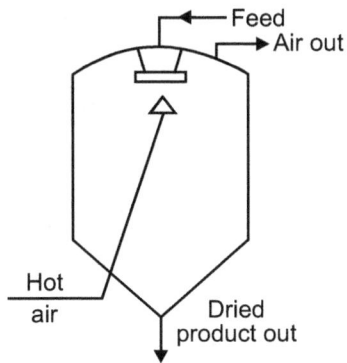

Spray dryer

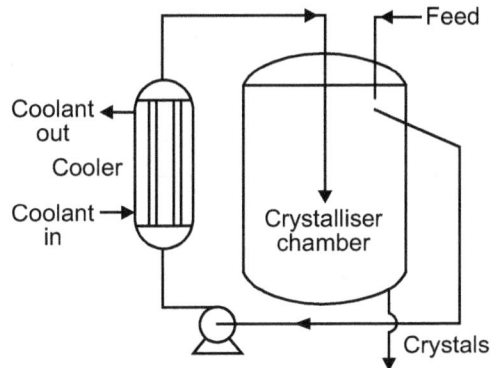

Oslo cooling crystalliser

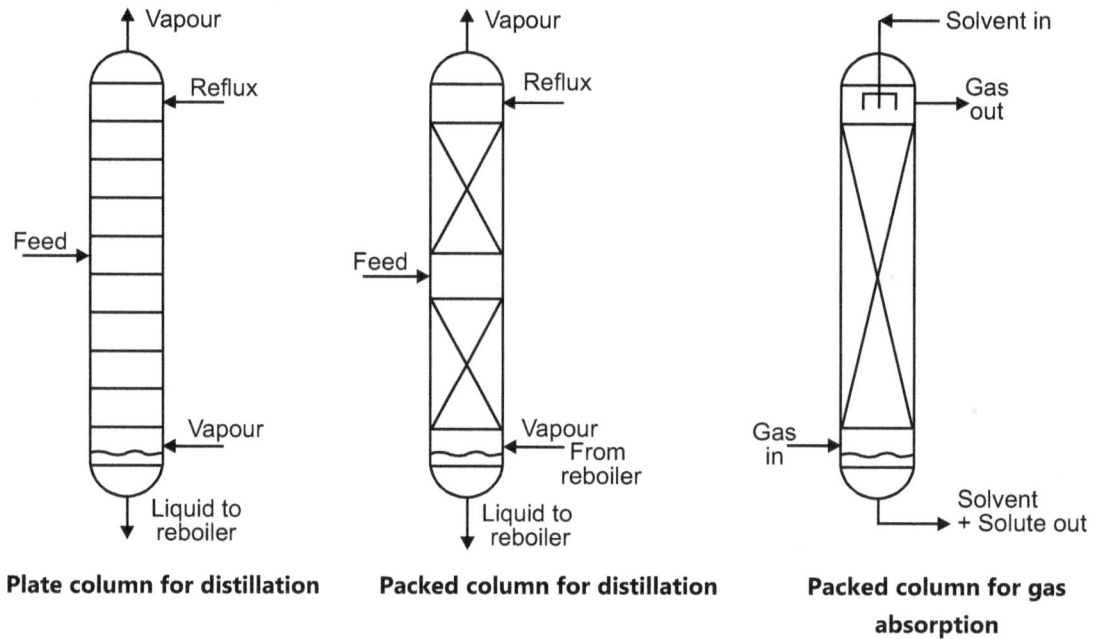

Plate column for distillation   Packed column for distillation   Packed column for gas absorption

Fig. 7.26 : Schematic views of process equipments

Graphical symbols for P and I diagrams :

IS : 9446-1980 lays down the symbols used in P and I diagrams for the chemical industries

1. **Valves and Fittings :**

Sr. No.	Description	Symbols
1.	Gate valve	
2.	Globe valve	
3.	Check valve	
4.	Diaphram valve	
5.	Safety valve	
6.	Ball valve	
7.	Solenoid valve (two way)	
8.	Solenoid valve (three way)	
9.	Butterfly valve	
10.	Regulating globe valve	
11.	Plug valve	

12.	Control valve	
13.	Needle valve	
14.	Electrically operated control valve	
15.	Multiway valve	
16.	Pinch valve	
17.	Rupture disc	
18.	Expansion joint	
19.	Hose connector	
20.	Line blind	
21.	Blank flange	
22.	Drain funnel	
23.	Cap	
24.	Venturimeter	
25.	Orifice meter	
26.	Rotameter	
27.	Vent	
28.	Traced lines	
29.	Jacketed lines	
30.	Insulation	
31.	Sight glass	

32.	Steam trap	
33.	Strainer Y-type	

2. Instrumentation symbols : Instrument signal lines :

34.	Instrument air signal	
35.	Instrument electric leads	
36.	Instrument capillary tubing	
37.	Hydraulic lines	—H—H—H—

3. Instrument symbols :

38.	Locally mounted instruments	
39.	Instrument mounted main panel	
40.	Instrument mounted local panel	
41.	Transmitted, locally mounted	
42.	Transmitter, panel mounted	
43.	Instrument identification	

Main panel means that the instrument is located on a panel in the control room.

Example :

•   Unit (plant) No. 09.

•   Temperature indicator and controller

•   Locally mounted.

•   Instrument No. 100.

4. Process Variable Symbols :

44.	Pressure	P
45.	Temperature	T
46.	Level	L
47.	Flow	F
48.	Density	D
49.	Weight	W
50.	Viscosity	V
51.	Quality analysis or concentration	Q

| 52. | H_2 ion concentration | pH |
| 53. | Speed | S |

5.   Instrument Function Symbols :

54.	Indicator	I
55.	Controller	C
56.	Recorder	R
57.	Integrator	S
58.	Alarms	A

Example :

H
(TA)

| • | High and low temperature alarm | L |

6.   Service fluid code :

59.	Instrument air	IA
60.	Plant air	PA
61.	Process air	PRA
62.	Inert gas	IG
63.	Fuel gas	FG
64.	Blow down	BD
65.	Drain	DR
66.	Raw water	RW
67.	Demineralised water	DMW
68.	Cooling water	CW or CTW
69.	Process water	PW
70.	Hot water	HW
71.	Chilled water	CHW
72.	Steam	S
73.	Condensate	C
74.	Refrigeration	R
75.	Nitrogen	N
76.	Fuel oil	FO
77.	Examples :	

Cooling water inflow header	——	CW	——
Cooling water return header	——	CWR	——
Cooling tower water inflow header	——	CTW	——
Cooling tower water return header	——	CTWR	——
Low press steam header	——	LPS	——
Condensate header	——	C	——

| Fuel oil inflow header | — | FOF | — |
| Fuel oil return header | — | FOR | — |

A point at which measurement is done is called as point of measurement.

A device that ascertains the magnitude of physical quantity or condition is called an instrument.

An instrument in which the value of the measured quantity/condition/parameter is displayed at the time of measurement (but not retained for subsequent reference) is called an Indicator.

An instrument in which the value of the measured parameter is retained for subsequent reference is called a recorder.

The control loops and instruments for measuring a particular parameter for a particular piece of an equipment (as per requirement) should be shown in P & I diagram
as per the diagrams to follow. Temperature, flow, level and pressure are the parameters that are usually controlled.

Instrument symbol comprises of a thin circle of approximately 10 mm diameter. A short continuous thin line is used to show connection from the point of measurement to the instrument symbol and it shall be normal to the flow line or vessel.

Fig. 7.27

Example showing position of identification (identifying) numbers and letters :

Fig. 7.28

Examples of use of symbols :

1. Flow rate indicator (locally mounted)

2. Flow recorder (locally mounted)

3. Level indicator (locally mounted)

4. pH recorder (main panel mounted)

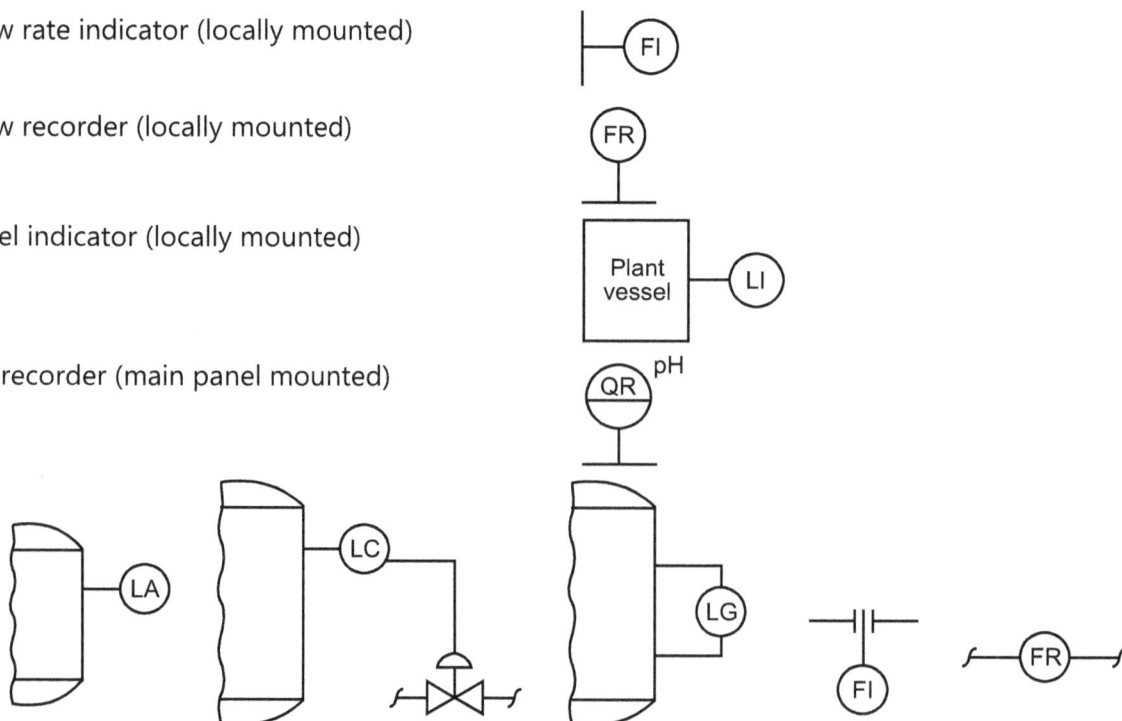

Level alarm internal type	Blind level internal type	Gauge glass	Differential type flow indicator	Flow recorder rotameter

Fig. 7.29

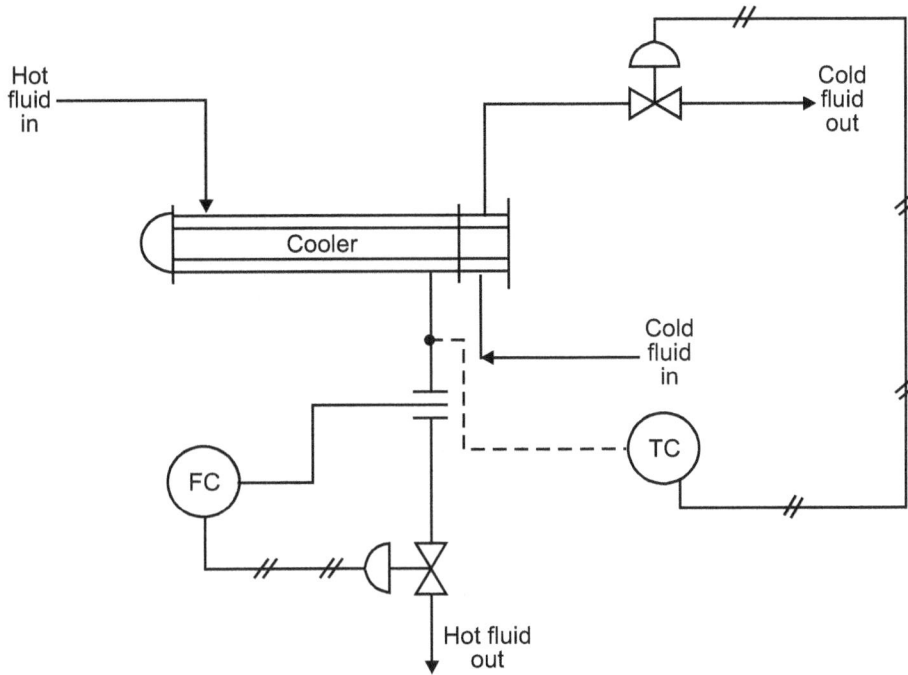

Fig. 7.30 : Cooler-temperature control

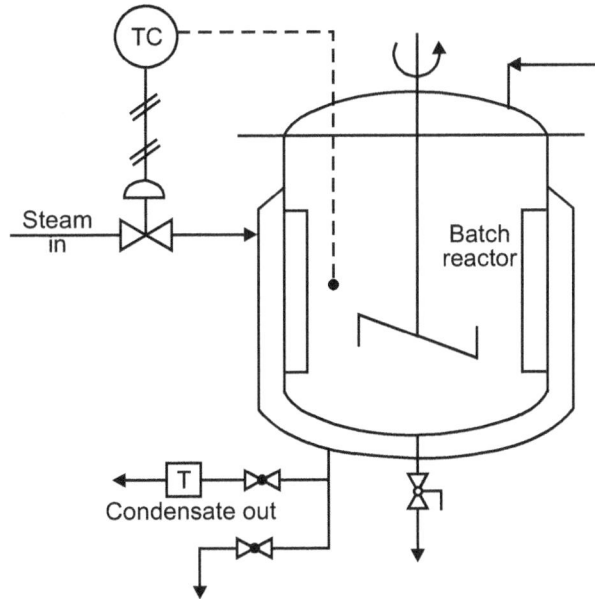

Fig. 7.31 : Reactor temperature control

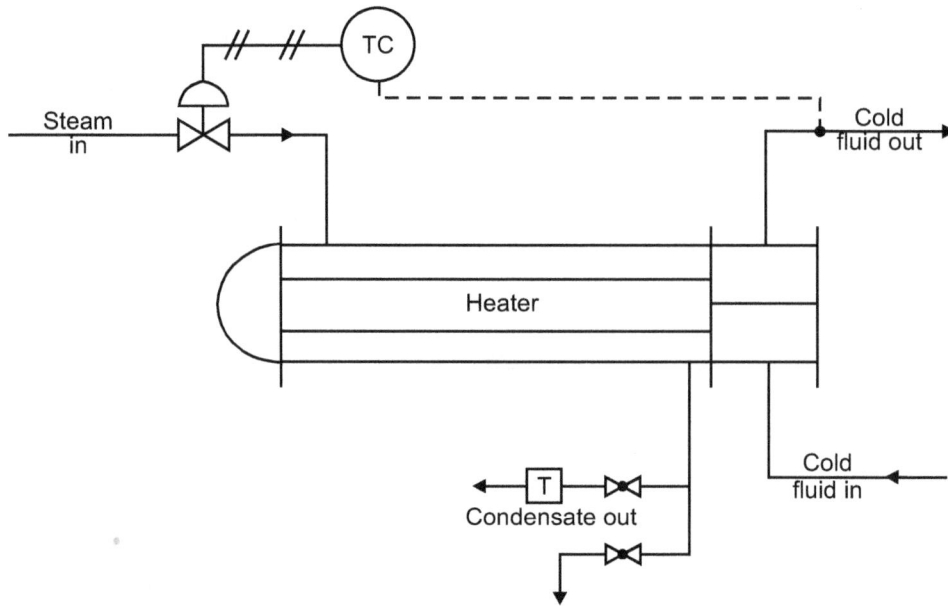

Fig. 7.32 : Heater-temperature control

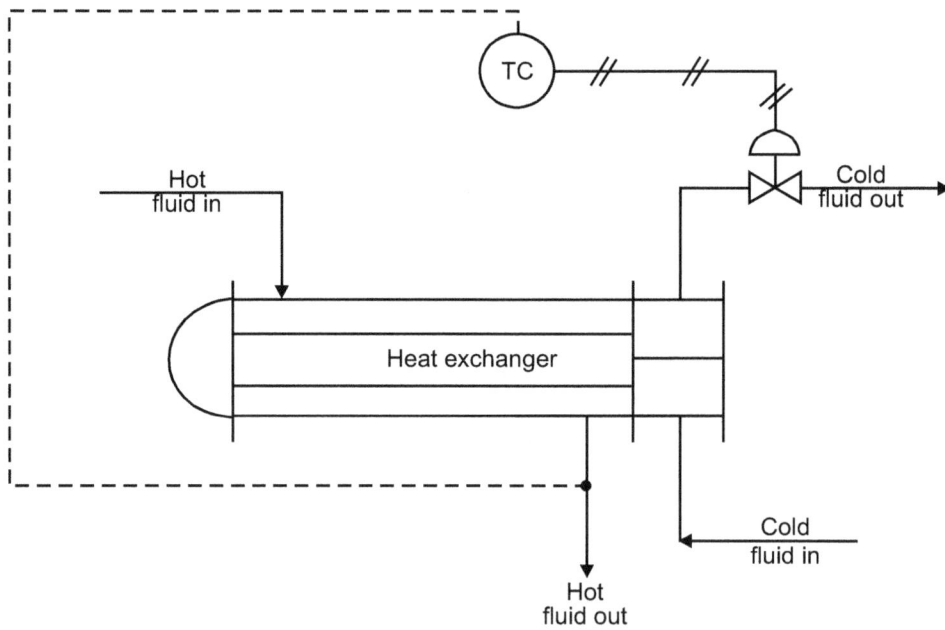

Fig. 7.33 : Hot fluid temperature control

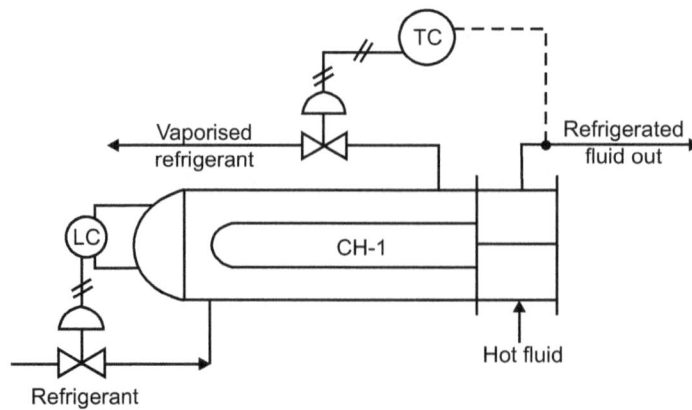

Fig. 7.34 : Control of chiller

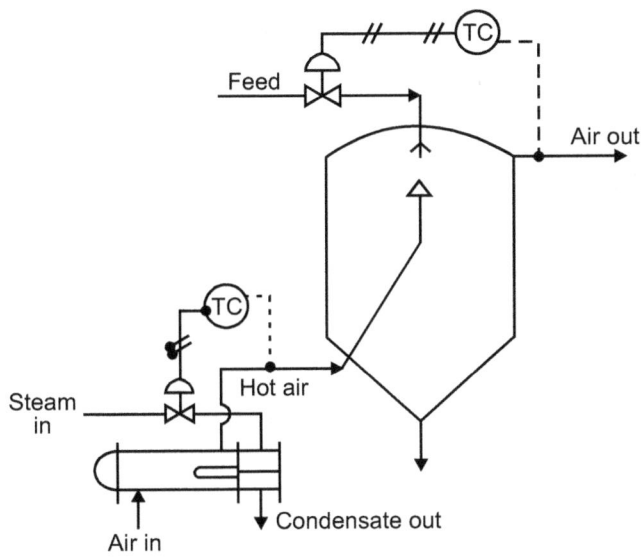

Fig. 7.35 : Spray dryer controller

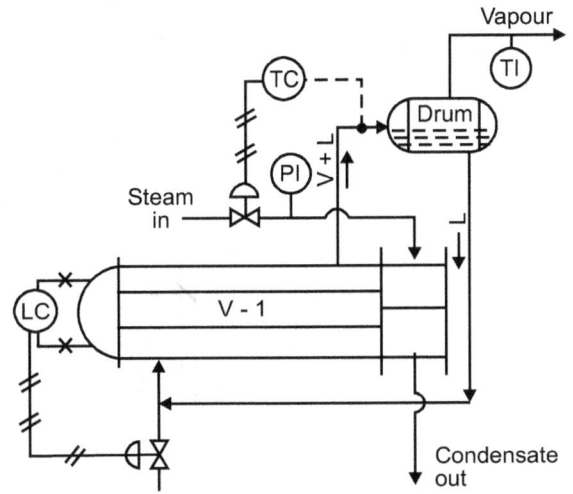

Fig. 7.36 : Control of vaporiser

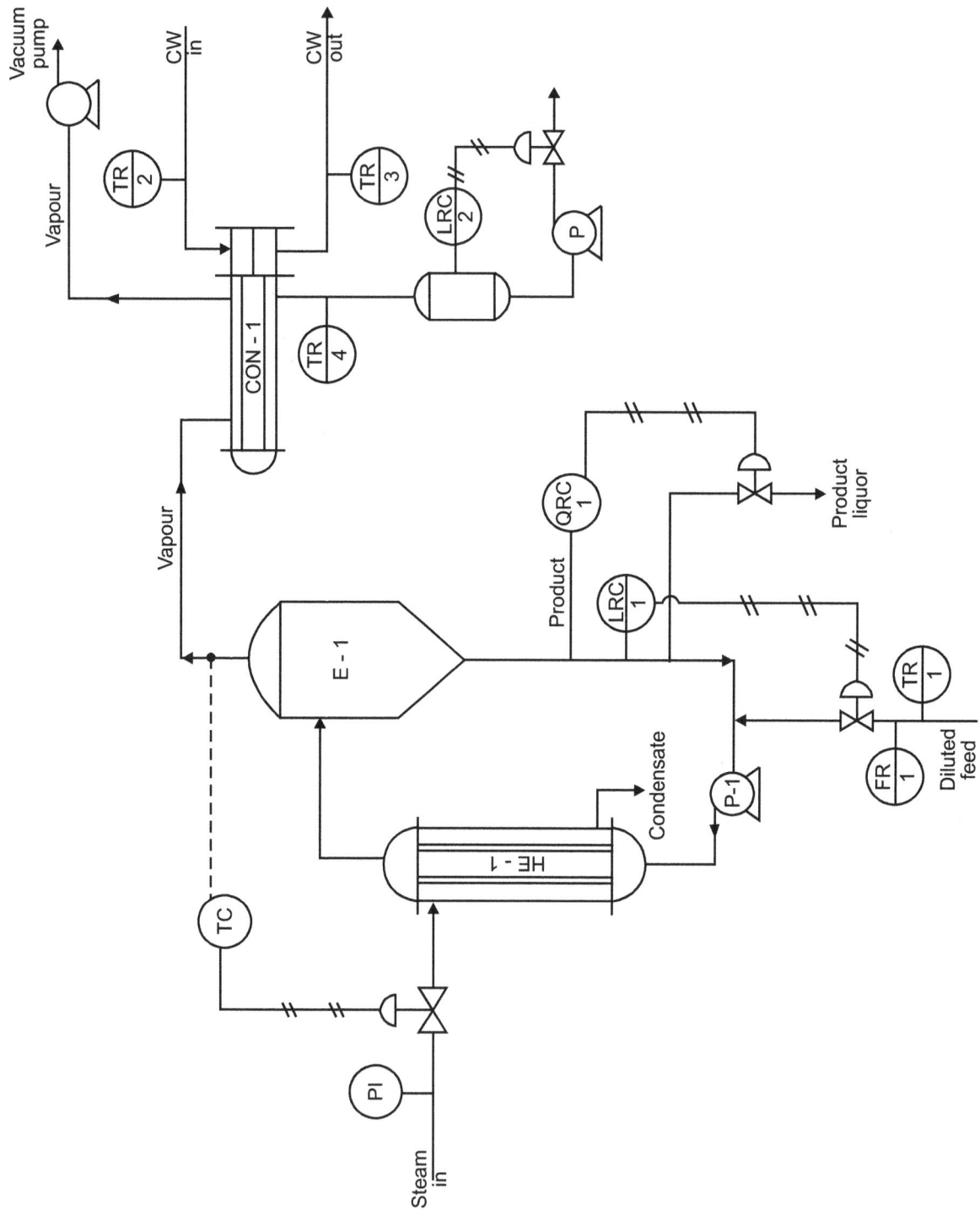

Fig. 7.37 : Forced circulation evaporator control (Vertical heating element)

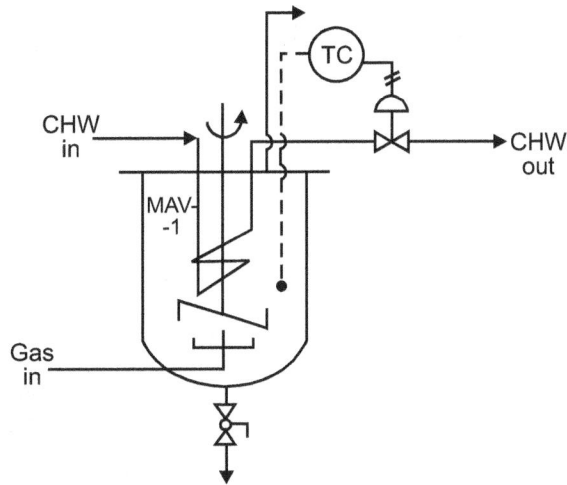

Fig. 7.38 : Control of mechanically agitated vessel used for gas absorption

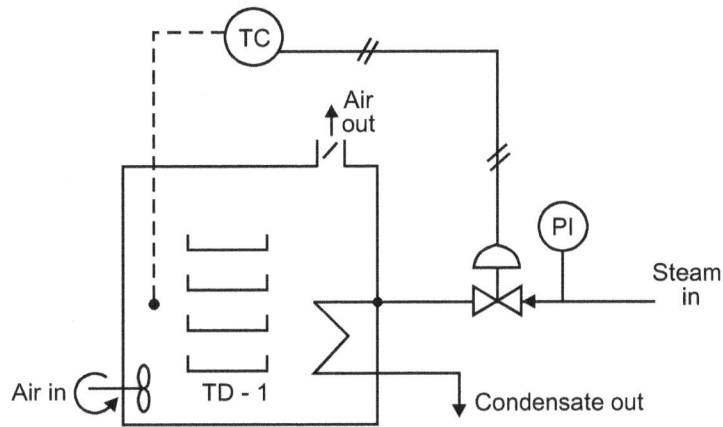

Fig. 7.39 : Control of tray dryer

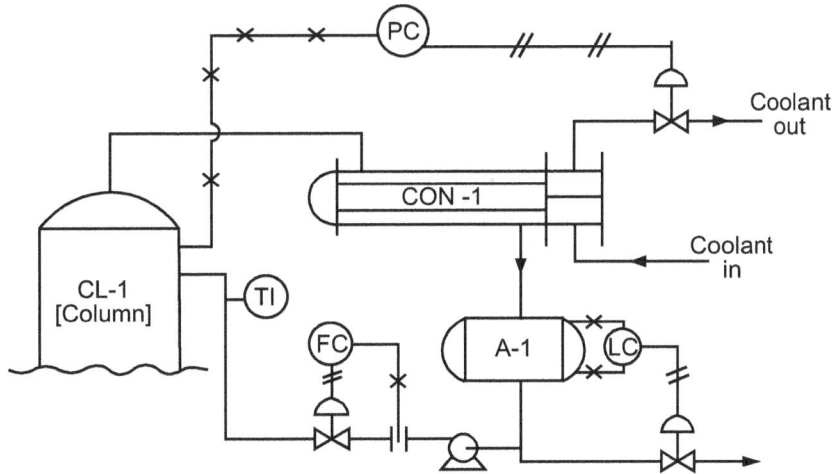

Fig. 7.40 : Tower pressure control

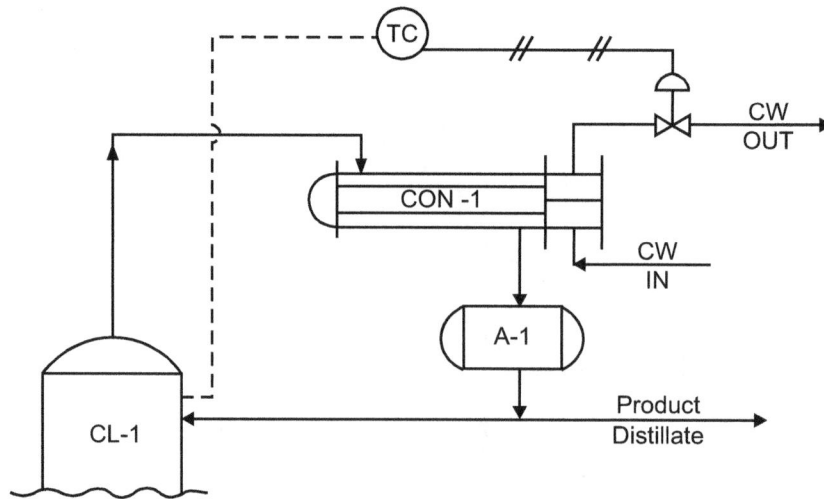

Fig. 7.41 : Top temperature control

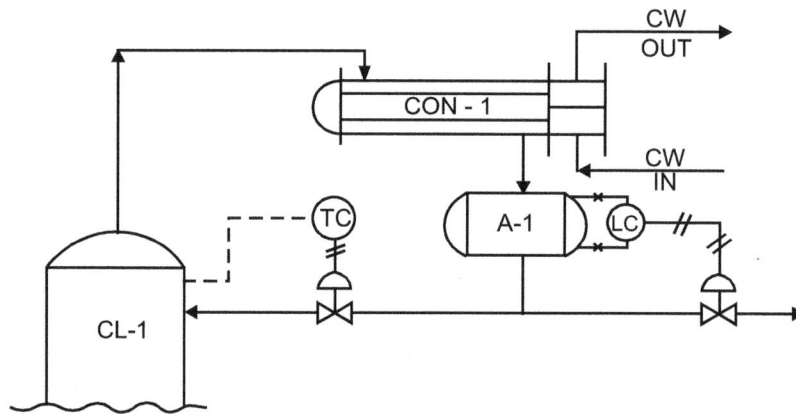

Fig. 7.42 : Top temperature control and accumulator level control

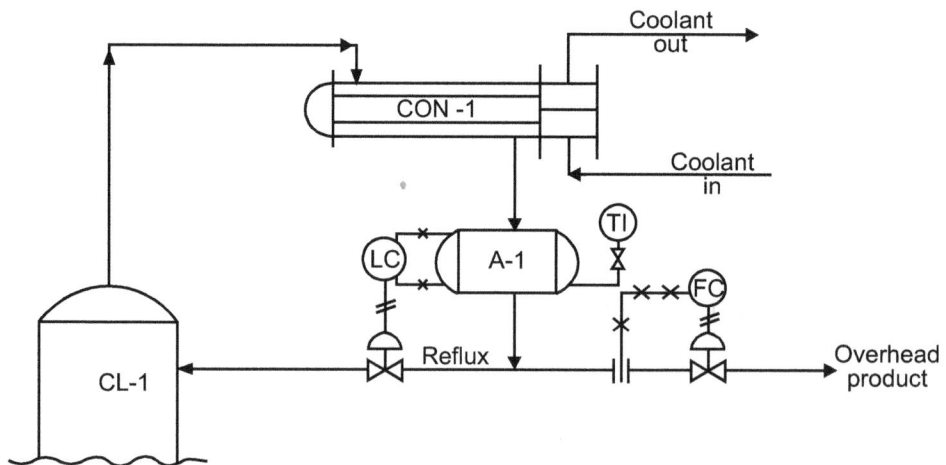

Fig. 7.43 : Control of level-accumulator with gravity flow or reflux

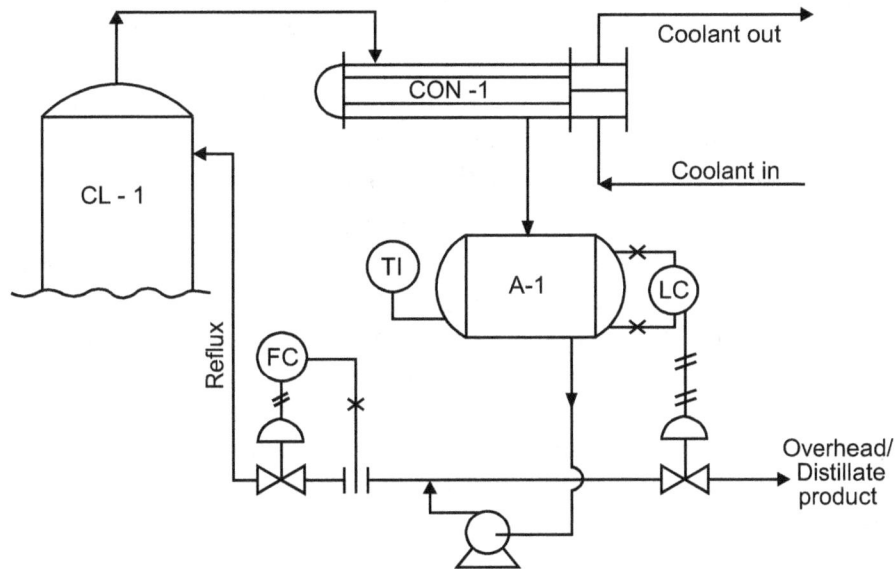

Fig. 7.44 : Control of level of accumulator and reflux condenser with pumped reflux

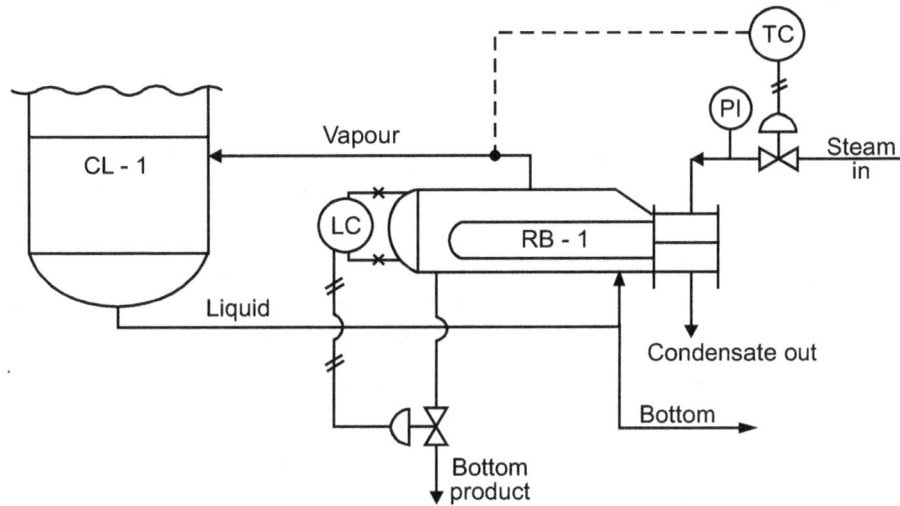

Fig. 7.45 : Steam flow rate and level control of reboiler

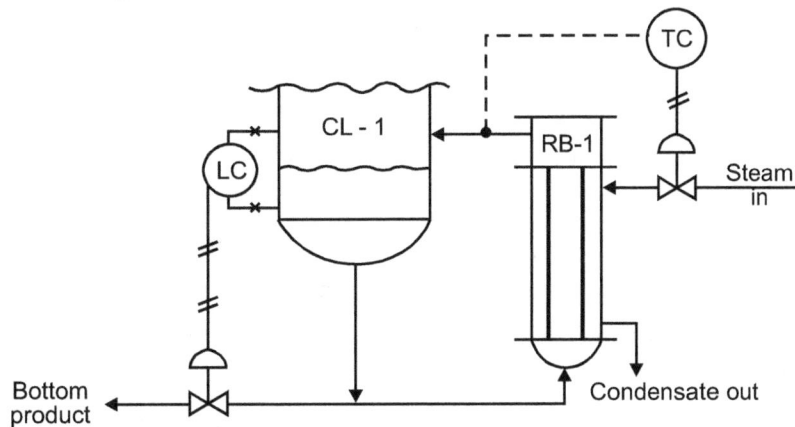

Fig. 7.46 : Vertical thermosyphon type reboiler-level and steam flow rate control of reboiler

7.3 EQUIPMENT LAYOUT

The equipment layout is based on the P and I diagram (Engineering Line Diagram). Once the ELD is prepared, the process equipment layout is undertaken. From the ELD of a process, we know the floor-wise installation of each equipment.

The process equipment layout shows the exact floor-wise placing of the equipments in a processing area. While making a layout, ample space should be assigned to each piece of equipment and equipments are so placed that they should be easily accessible for maintenance. We have to do the placing of equipments so as to minimise-damage to persons, property in case of fire, explosion, etc., maintenance cost, number of persons required to operate the plant, construction costs, and cost of planned future expansion.

There two ways of laying out a processing area, namely, grouped layout and flow line layout. The grouped layout places all similar pieces of equipment adjacent. With this type of arrangement, switching from one unit to another is possible. This arrangement provides ease of operation and we can reduce the requirement of operators as one or two operators can supervise all equipments of a like nature. For instance, if there are 7 batch reactors, these would all be placed in same general area, and could be watched by a minimum of operators; if they were spread out over a wide area, more operators might be required. The grouped layout is best suited for large plants. The flow line layout utilises train or line system, which places all the equipments in the order/sequence as it appears in the process flow sheet. This type of layout thus minimises the length of transfer lines and consequently reduces the energy required to transport materials. It is generally adopted for small plants.

Instead of using the grouped layout or flow line layout alone, a combination of these two types that best suits the specific situation is often used. Detailed layout of processing area is helpful and necessary in determining the first realistic estimates of routing, lengths, and sequence of piping.

The equipment layout gives us idea regarding the exact location of a process equipment on the floor on which it is placed.

In the chemical industry, the cost of maintenance is very large and one has to always think of reducing this cost. Adequate space must be kept around all equipment so that it can be easily serviced and operated (e.g., a floating head heat exchanger must have enough clear space so that we can very easily remove the tube bundle out of the shell and take it elsewhere for repairs). In case of vessels containing coils and agitators we have to provide enough headroom for taking these components out of the vessel. The operations involving possibility of fire or explosion hazards should be physically separated from the rest of the operations (should be located in a separate area). The road should be provided around the perimeter of the site and no roads should deadend.

The process equipment layout, i.e., layout of a processing area should be drawn floor wise. For drawing this diagram, we have to refer to the ELD drawn which gives idea regarding the floor-wise installation of process equipments, etc. When dimensions of the process equipments are given then the layout of processing area should be drawn to scale. When dimensions are not given then suitable proportionate sizes of equipments should be assumed for drawing a layout. The layout of processing area gives us idea regarding the exact location of a process equipment on a particular floor.

While making a process equipment layout :

(i)   Keep a distance of at least 750 mm - 1000 mm between any two adjacent equipments - to have ease in moving around the equipments and to attend any maintenance work.

(ii)   A clear-cut distane of 750-1000 mm should be kept vacant from all four walls of the factory building.

(iii)   Refer to the P and I diagram/LED to get idea regarding floor-wise installation of the equipments.

        (The equipments placed on the ground floor in the ELD will only appear in the layout drawing of the ground floor of the processing area.)

(iv)   Before drawing the layout make a perfect decision regarding exact locations of the equipments on each floor.

(v)   In the layout drawing vertical process equipments will be represented by circles and horizontal equipments will be represented by rectangles. We have to draw circles for vertical equipments as the top view of a vertical cylindrical equipment is a circle while the top view/plan of horizontal cylindrical equipment is a rectangle.

(vi)   Start with the ground floor layout. Mark x-y coordinate axes in the bottom portion of a drawing sheet indicating two sides of the ground floor. Mark a boundary of
750-1000 mm along these axes as free space.

While drawing circles and rectangles as per the plans of the process equipments along x or y coordinate, draw first a centre line for all the equipments in one row considering the largest circle or rectangle representing the largest vertical or horizontal equipment (diameterwise) in that row so that this circle or rectangle touches the boundary line previously drawn. All other circles and rectangles representing the equipments involved are drawn along the same centre line keeping a distance of 750-1000 mm between adjacent equipments.

Once plans of all the equipments are drawn, fix lengths of the x and y axes such that the length of x or y axis beyond the last plan along x or y axis is 1000 mm. These x and y axes indicate two sides of the ground floor. Draw the remaining two sides to complete the layout of the ground floor. Then proceed to draw a layout of the first floor and so on.

If a process equipment is occupying a space of the ground as well as the first floor then it will appear in the layout both the floors at the same direction.

Tank farm and utility block diagram can be coupled with layout of a processing area.
In this case (i.e., in coupling these diagrams), the utility block diagram is drawn on one side and the tank farm is drawn on the other side of the equipment layout of the ground floor.

When we have to draw a layout of the ground floor, we have to imagine that we are on the first floor, assume the floor to be transparent and we are looking at the ground floor and so on. The equipments which actually occupy the floor space of a particular floor should only be drawn in the layout of that floor. For instance, if a reactor is embedded in the first floor and projected to the ground floor then it should be drawn/shown in the layout of first floor. If the distillation column of say 9 meter height is involved in a given process and the floor to floor distance is 6 meters, then the column should appear as a circle in the layout of ground as well as the layout of first floor at the same location.

In addition to the equipments, pumps, etc. one has to show the shift incharge cabin, laboratory, stair case, etc. in the layout drawing.

7.4 TANK FARM

A place nearby the processing area or some distance away from the processing area and located away from the utility generating units, e.g., a boiler house where liquid raw materials, solvents, and finished products are stored in storage tanks (located at one place) is called tank farm. These storage tanks are kept open to sky and bonded by brick wall called dike wall.

Liquids such as sulphuric acid, hydrochloric acid, nitric acid etc. could be stored in tanks which can be located /placed nearby the processing area to reduce materials handling. Storage tanks for flammable liquids such as acetone, benzene, etc. are located at a distance of 30 meter away from the processing area to avoid the danger of damage to the main plant due to fire in storage tanks. For flammable liquids such as benzene, cyclohexane, etc., it is also a practice to use underground storage tanks. In case of underground storage tanks, pumps are on the ground floor with self priming facilities for transport of materials to the processing area.

Vertical storage tanks are used for bulk storage of liquid materials as petroleum products, sulphuric acid, hydrochloric acid, etc. For storage of liquid products in small quantities as well as for underground storage of flammable liquids, horizontal tanks are used. Horizontal tanks are also used for intermediate storage of semifinished materials in the processing area. For storage of large volume under moderate pressures, spherical or horizontal cylindrical vessels are used. For storage of gas (atmospheric storage) vertical cylindrical tanks such as gas holders are used. For storage of gas under moderate pressures, spherical tanks (spheres) are used. For high pressure storage, cylindrical type pressure vessels are more economical due to reduction in volume. Multispheres (two) are also used for storage of gas under moderate pressures. For storage of solid materials silo, bins, bunkers etc. are used. Valuable solid materials are packed in drum or bags and stored in a godown/warehouse.

In the tank farm drawing - vertical cylindrical storage tanks and spheres are represented by circles and horizontal storage tanks are represented by rectangles. Vertical storage tanks are used for storing large quantity of liquid materials as compared to horizontal storage tanks. Therefore, the circle representing a vertical storage tank is to be drawn larger in size (diameterwise) than the rectangle representing a horizontal tank.

Pumps are to be represented by small rectangles. The minimum distance between - adjacent tanks, tank and pump, two pumps, tank and dike wall should be 750-1000 mm.

We have to draw circles and/or rectangles of various sizes as per requirements for the tanks involved along a centre line, which should be a straight line (tank farm layout should not be drawn zig-zag). Small rectangles for the pumps involved are to be drawn along the centre line drawn. If only one pump is involved then it should be shown by a small rectangle on the centre line and if two pumps are involved (on-line pump and stand-by pump), they are represented by two rectangles on either sides of the centre line. It is usual practice to show three pumps nearby a raw material storage tank - two pumps (on-line and stand-by pumps) to transfer the raw material from the tank to the processing area and one pump for unloading tankers (for transferring the raw material from the tanker into the storage tank). We have to show only one pump nearby a finished product storage tank - it is to be used for loading tankers (i.e., for transferring the finished product from the storage tank into the tankers).

In any chemical plant, the process equipments are of smaller sizes (diameterwise) compared to the storage tanks. Therefore, circles and rectangles in the tank farm drawing of the plant are to be drawn larger in size compared to circles and rectangles appearing in the equipment layout.

It is usual practice to couple the tank farm drawing of a plant with the equipment layout of the ground floor of the same plant.

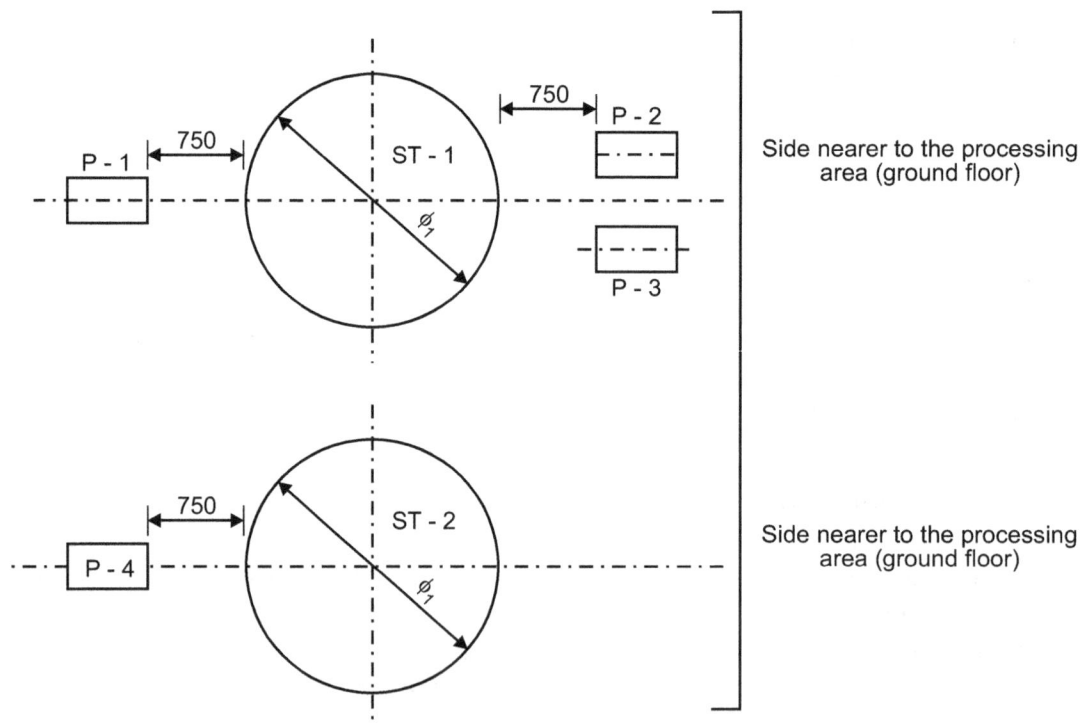

Fig. 7.47

Code	Description
ST - 1 -	Storage tank for raw material.
P-1 P-2, P-3	Transfer pumps.
P-1	Pump for unloading tankers
P-2 and P-3	Raw material transfer pumps to processing area.

| ST - 2 | Storage tank for finished product. |
| P - 4 | Pump for loading tankers with finished product |

Fig. 7.47 shows a method of representation of vertical storage tanks and transfer pumps for a raw material and finished product in the tank farm drawing.

Fig. 7.51 and Fig. 7.55 show typical tank form drawings.

Ex. 7.11 : Oxalic acid is to be produced by oxidation of sugar. A mixed acid is prepared in a mechanically agitated vessel (MAV), incorporating a cooling coil, out of sulphuric acid, nitric acid and water. Catalyst V_2O_5 is added in this vessel. Cooling tower water (CTW) is used as a cooling medium during preparation of the acid. The mixed acid is transferred to a jacketed batch reactor and sugar is added slowly to the reactor under agitation over a predetermined period. The oxidation reaction is exothermic and reaction temperature is 55 - 60°C. Temperature is maintained at 60°C by circulating CTW through the jacket during the course of reaction.

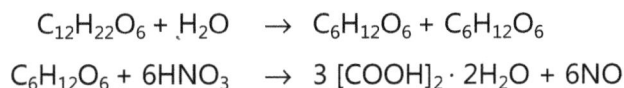

$$C_{12}H_{22}O_6 + H_2O \rightarrow C_6H_{12}O_6 + C_6H_{12}O_6$$

$$C_6H_{12}O_6 + 6HNO_3 \rightarrow 3[COOH]_2 \cdot 2H_2O + 6NO$$

'NO' gas liberated during the course of reaction is fed from the top of reactor to an oxidiser (simply a double pipe arrangement type) to convert NO to NO_2 with the help of air. CTW is used as a cooling medium to the oxidiser. Gases containing NO_2 from the oxidiser are fed to a battery of absorption towers in series (2 Nos.) wherein NO_2 is absorbed in water to produce nitric acid. Unabsorbed gases are vented.

After the reaction is complete the mass in the reactor is cooled and is then transferred to a batch crystalliser (stir-tank crystalliser incorporating a cooling coil). Chilled water (CHW) is used as a utility for the crystalliser. Crystalliser is maintained at temperature of 15°C at which oxalic acid crystallises as oxalic acid dihydrate. The slurry of oxalic acid is then fed to a basket centrifuge to obtain wet oxalic acid. The wet oxalic acid is then dried in a tray dryer at 50°C to obtain the product oxalic acid.

The filtrate liquor from the centrifuge machine is collected in an intermediate storage tank. This filtrate containing water, HNO_3 etc. is to be used for the absorption of NO_2 in the absorption tower. Weak liquor containing HNO_3 from the storage tank is fed to the absorption tower via a chiller as the absorption of NO_2 in H_2O is exothermic. Chilled water is used as a utility for the chiller. Liquor from the storage tank goes to the chiller then to the absorption tower and from the bottom of tower to the storage tank, i.e., it is kept in circulation till the absorption of NO_2 is complete and which is to be used for a next batch for preparing the mixed acid required.

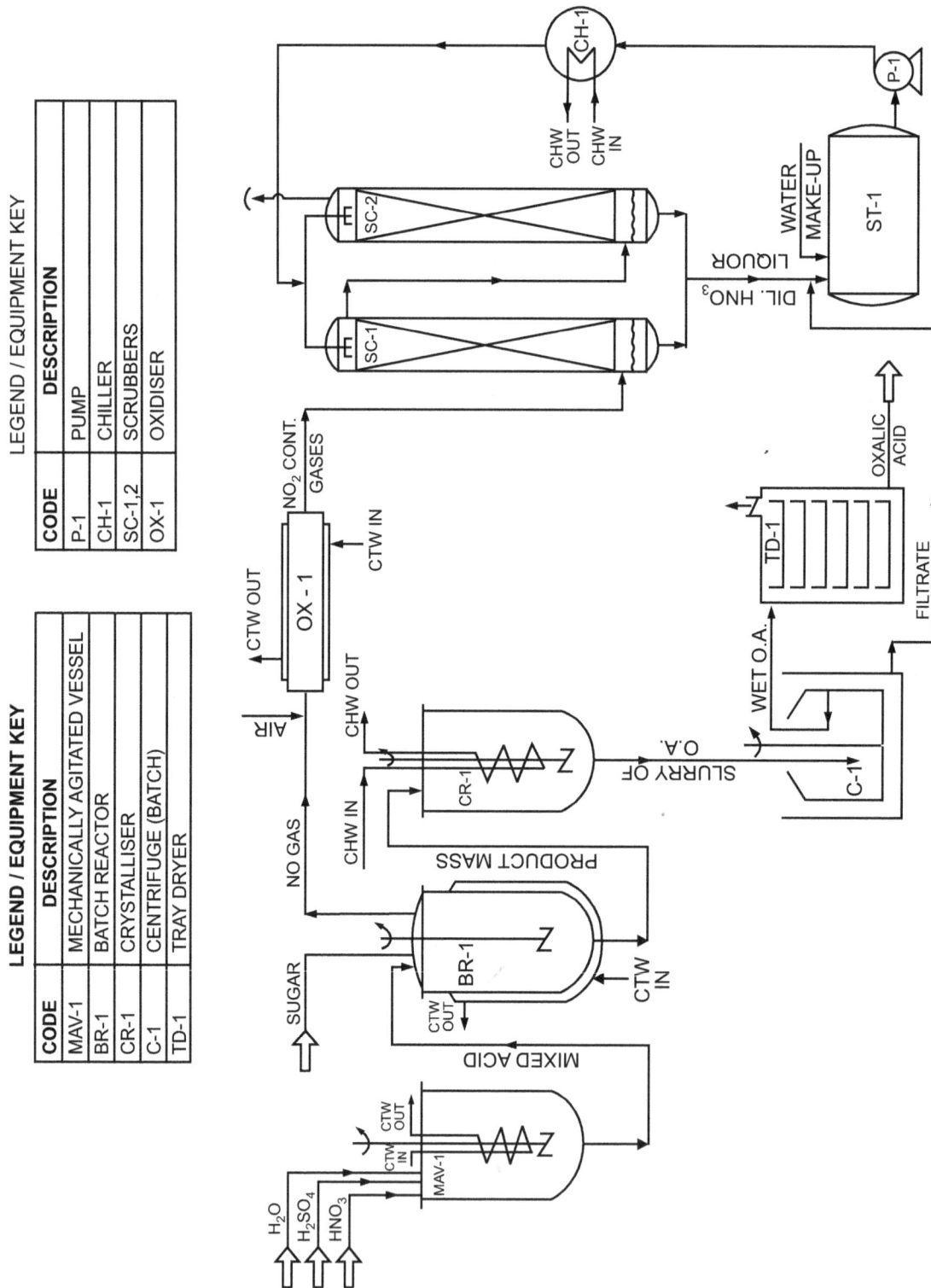

LEGEND / EQUIPMENT KEY

CODE	DESCRIPTION
P-1	PUMP
CH-1	CHILLER
SC-1,2	SCRUBBERS
OX-1	OXIDISER

LEGEND / EQUIPMENT KEY

CODE	DESCRIPTION
MAV-1	MECHANICALLY AGITATED VESSEL
BR-1	BATCH REACTOR
CR-1	CRYSTALLISER
C-1	CENTRIFUGE (BATCH)
TD-1	TRAY DRYER

FIG. 7.48 : PROCESS OF SHEET OF MANUFACTURE OF OXALIC ACID BY OXIDATION OF SUGAR

LEGEND / EQUIPMENT KEY

SYMBOL	DESCRIPTION
MAV-1	MECHANICAL AGITATED VESSEL
BR-1	BATCH REACTOR
CR-1	CRYSTALLISER
C-1	CENTRIFUGE

LEGEND / EQUIPMENT KEY

TD-1	TRAY DRYER
P-1	PUMP
CH-1	CHILLER
SC-1,2	SCRUBBERS
DX-1	OXIDISER
IST-1	INTERMEDIATE STORAGE TANK

	GLOBE
	BALL
	PLUG

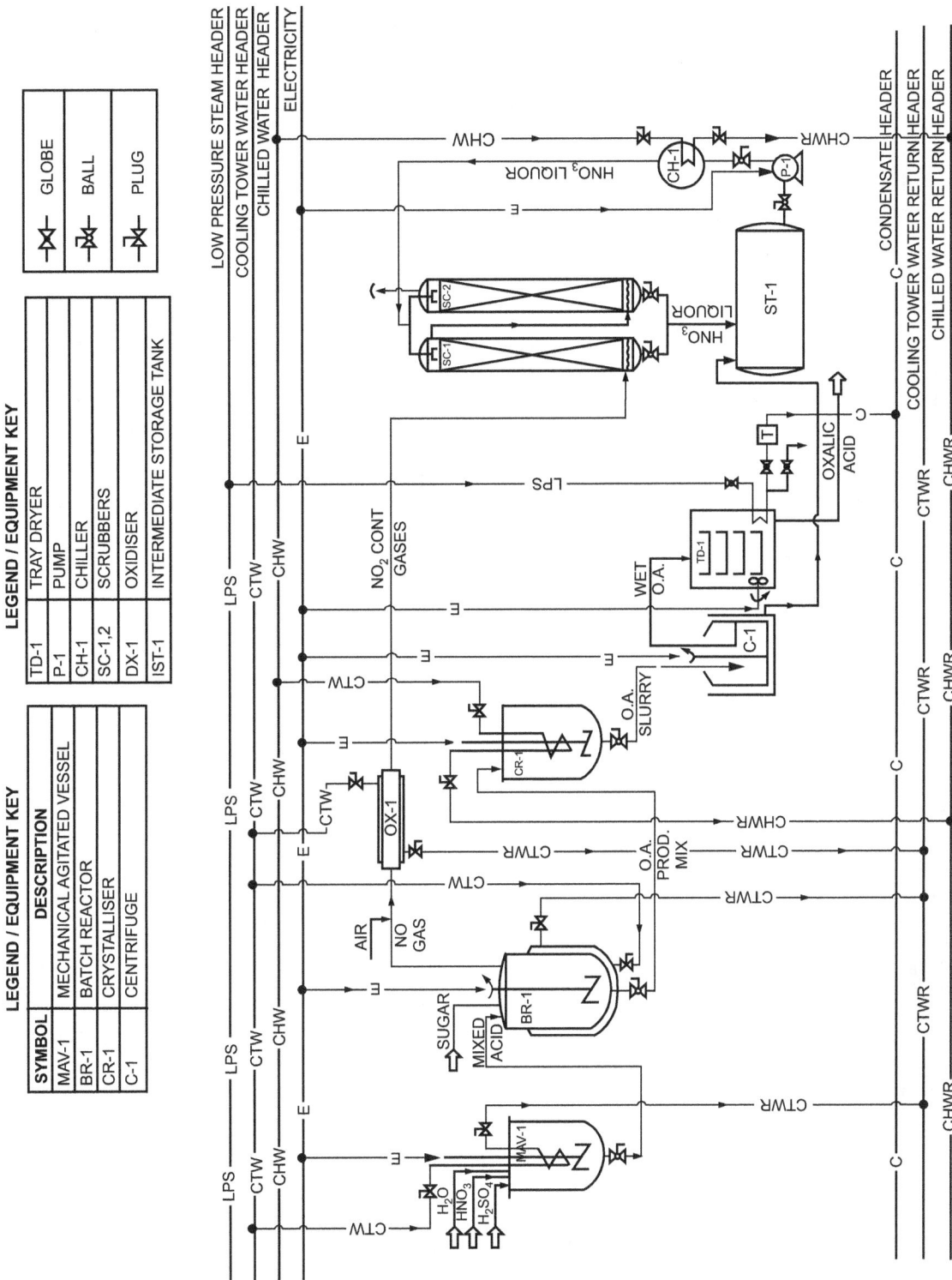

FIG. 7.49 : UTILITY LINE DIAGRAM-OXALIC ACID BY OXIDATION OF SUGAR

LEGEND/ EQUIPMENT KEY

CODE	DESCRIPTION
TD-1	TRAY DRIER
P-1-,3	PUMPS
CH-1	CHILLER
OX-1	OXIDISER
SC-1,2	SCRUBBERS

LEGEND/ EQUIPMENT KEY

CODE	DESCRIPTION
MAV-1	MECHANICAL AGITATED VESSEL
BR-1	BATCH REACTOR
CR-1	CRYSTALLISER
CF-1	CENTRIFUGE
GF	GROUND FLOOR
FF	FIRST FLOOR

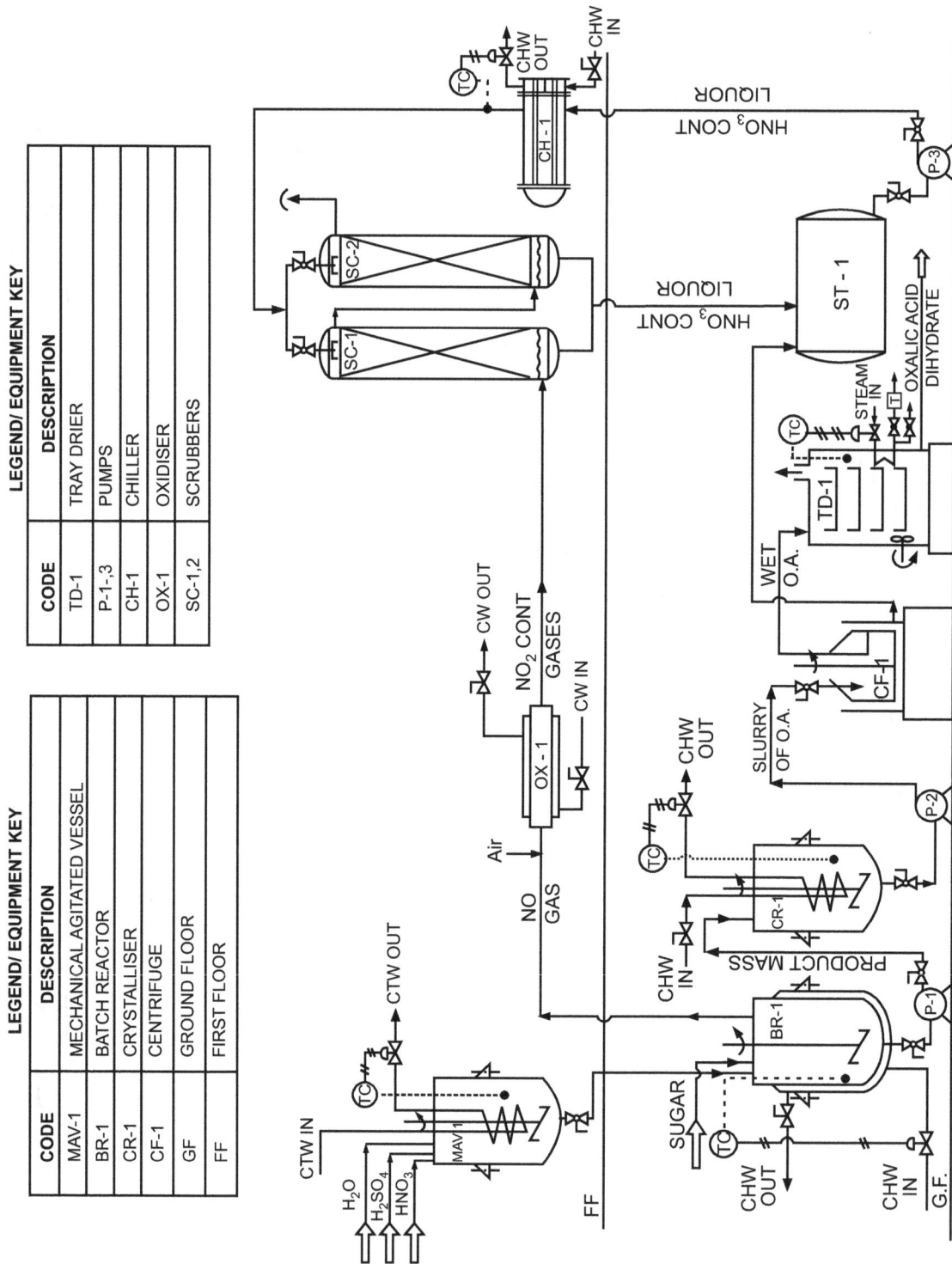

FIG. 7.50 : P & I DIAGRAM/ENGINEERING LINE DIAGRAM FOR OXALIC ACID MANUFACTURE BY OXIDATION OF SUGAR

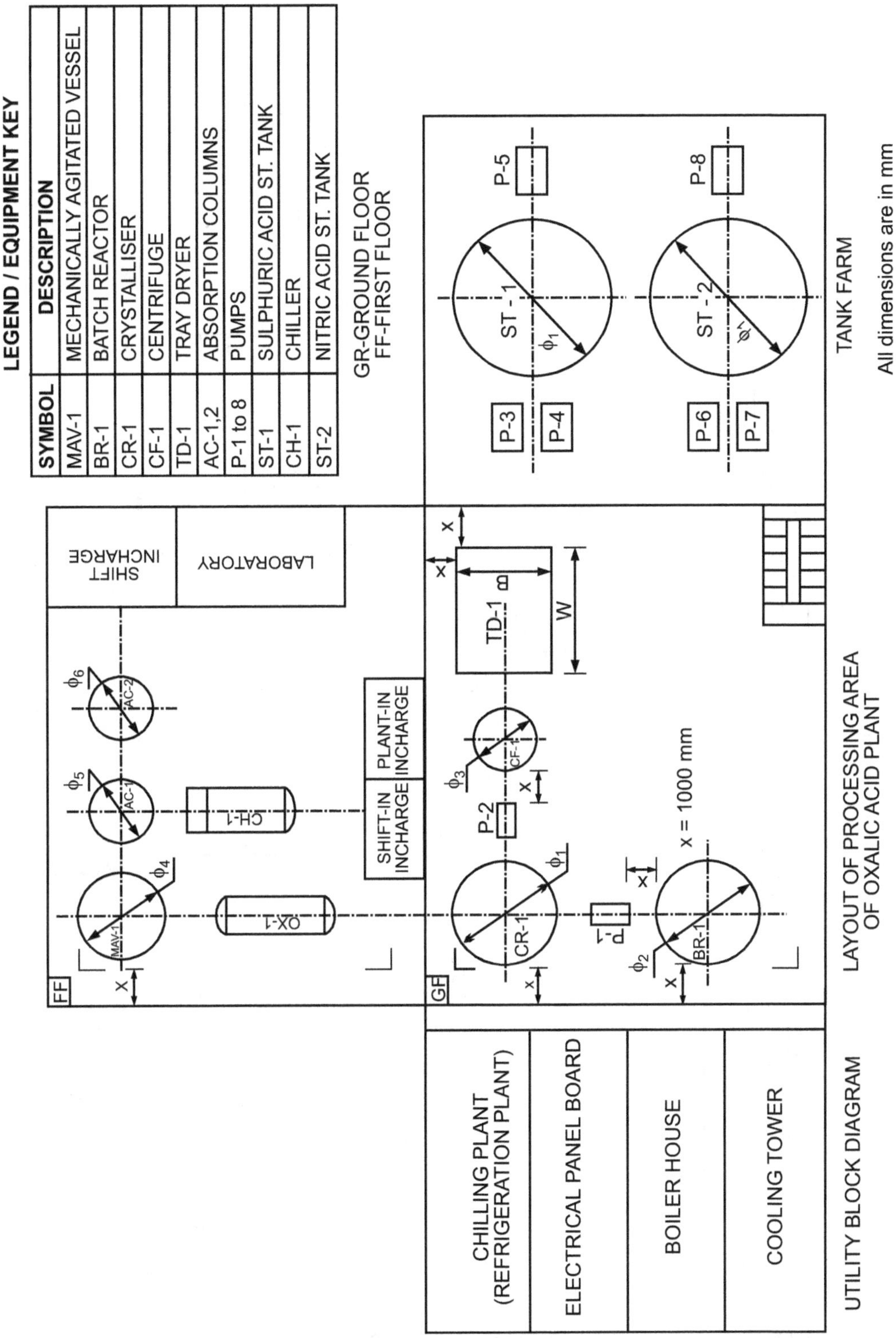
LEGEND / EQUIPMENT KEY
SYMBOL | DESCRIPTION
MAV-1 | MECHANICALLY AGITATED VESSEL
BR-1 | BATCH REACTOR
CR-1 | CRYSTALLISER
CF-1 | CENTRIFUGE
TD-1 | TRAY DRYER
AC-1,2 | ABSORPTION COLUMNS
P-1 to 8 | PUMPS
ST-1 | SULPHURIC ACID ST. TANK
CH-1 | CHILLER
ST-2 | NITRIC ACID ST. TANK
GR-GROUND FLOOR
FF-FIRST FLOOR
SHIFT INCHARGE
LABORATORY
FF
MAV-1
AC-1
AC-2
CH-1
OX-1
SHIFT-IN INCHARGE
PLANT-IN INCHARGE
GF
CR-1
BR-1
CF-1
TD-1
P-1
P-2
x = 1000 mm
P-3
P-4
P-5
P-6
P-7
P-8
ST - 1
ST - 2
TANK FARM
All dimensions are in mm
x = (750 – 1000 mm)
LAYOUT OF PROCESSING AREA OF OXALIC ACID PLANT
CHILLING PLANT (REFRIGERATION PLANT)
ELECTRICAL PANEL BOARD
BOILER HOUSE
COOLING TOWER
UTILITY BLOCK DIAGRAM

FIG. 7.51 : EQUIPMENT LAYOUT, TANK FARM, AND UBD OF OXALIC ACID

LEGEND / EQUIPMENT KEY

CODE	DESCRIPTION
A-1	ACCUMULATOR
ST-1	ETHYL ALCOHOL STORAGE TANK
PH-1	PREHEATER
P-1,2	PUMPS

LEGEND / EQUIPMENT KEY

CODE	DESCRIPTION
AC-1	AZEOTROPE COLUMN
RC-1	RECOVERY COLUMN
RB-1,2	REBOILERS (VERTICAL THERMOSYPHON)
CON-1,2	CONDENSERS
D-1	DECANTER

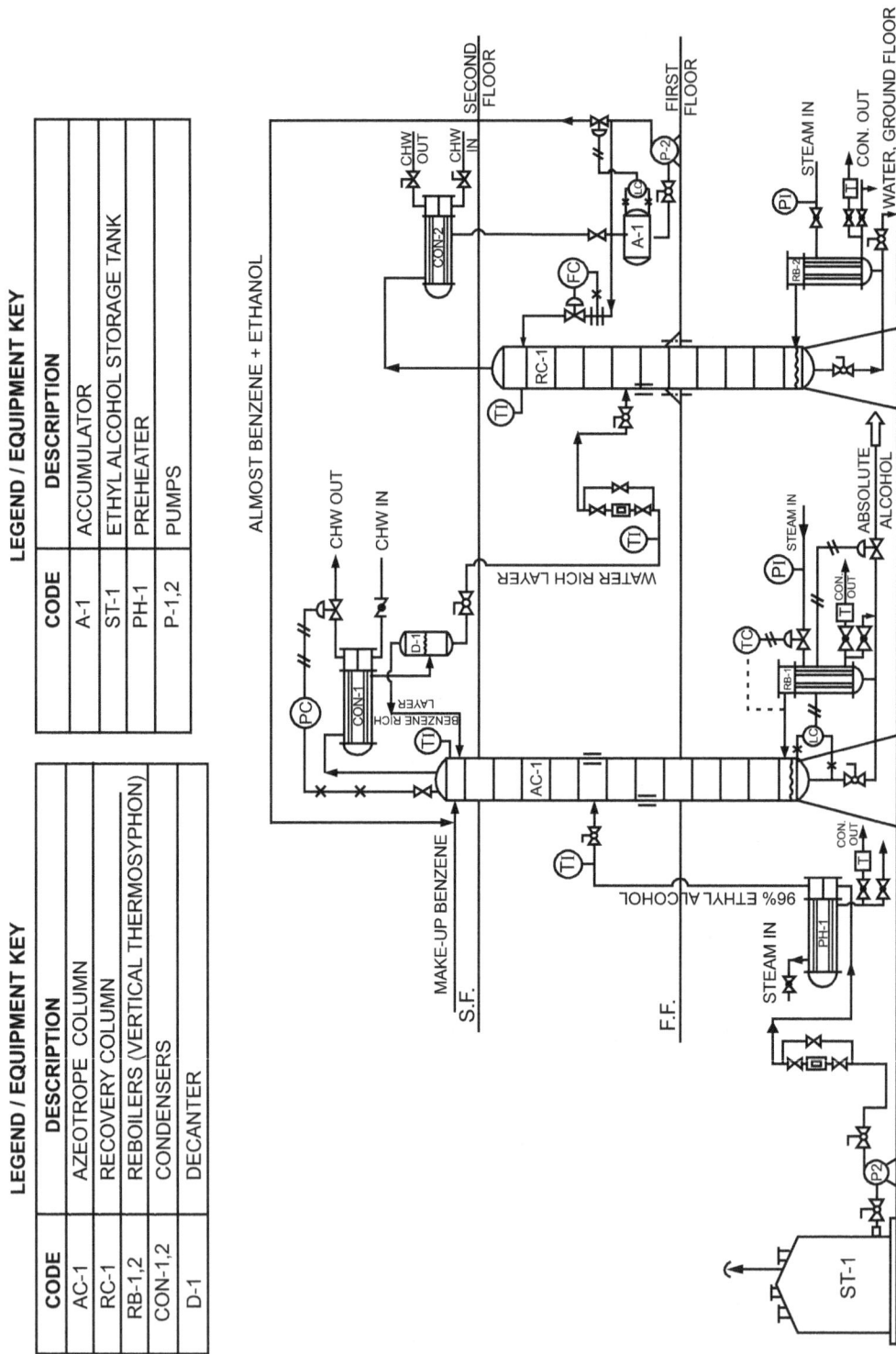

FIG. 7.52 : P & I DIAGRAM / ENGINEERING LINE DIAGRAM FOR PRODUCTION OF ABSOLUTE ALCOHOL BY AZEOTROPIC DISTILLATION OF 96% BY WT. ETHYL ALCOHOL

LEGEND / EQUIPMENT KEY

CODE	DESCRIPTION
BR-1	BATCH REACTOR
C-1	CENTRIFUGE
SC-1,2	SCRUBBERS
TD-1	TRAY DRYER
HM-1	HAMMER MILL
MAV-1	MECHANICALLY ACITATED VESSEL
P-1,2	PUMPS

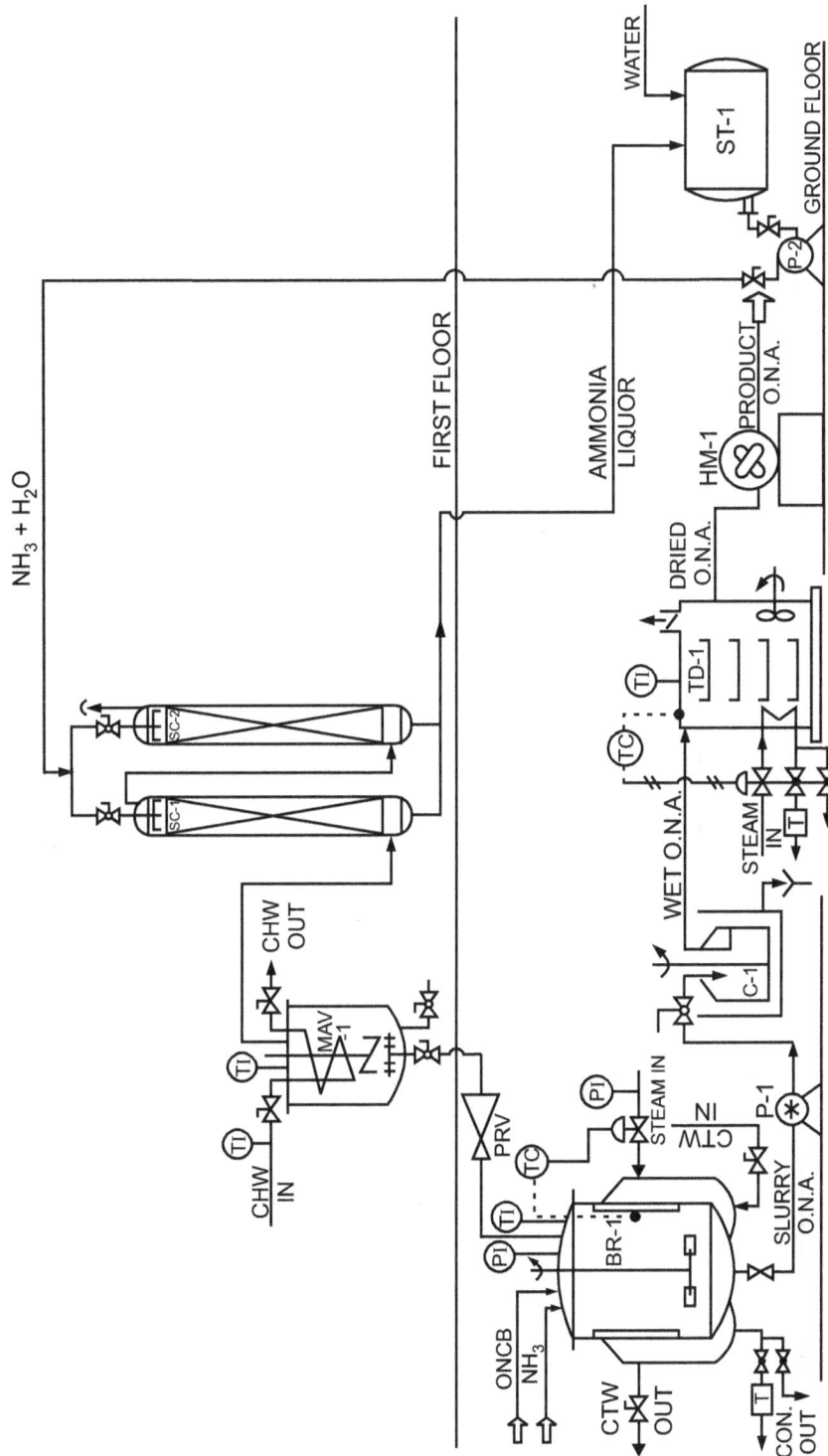

FIG. 7.53 : P & I DIAGRAM / ENGINEERING LINE DIAGRAM - ONA PLANT

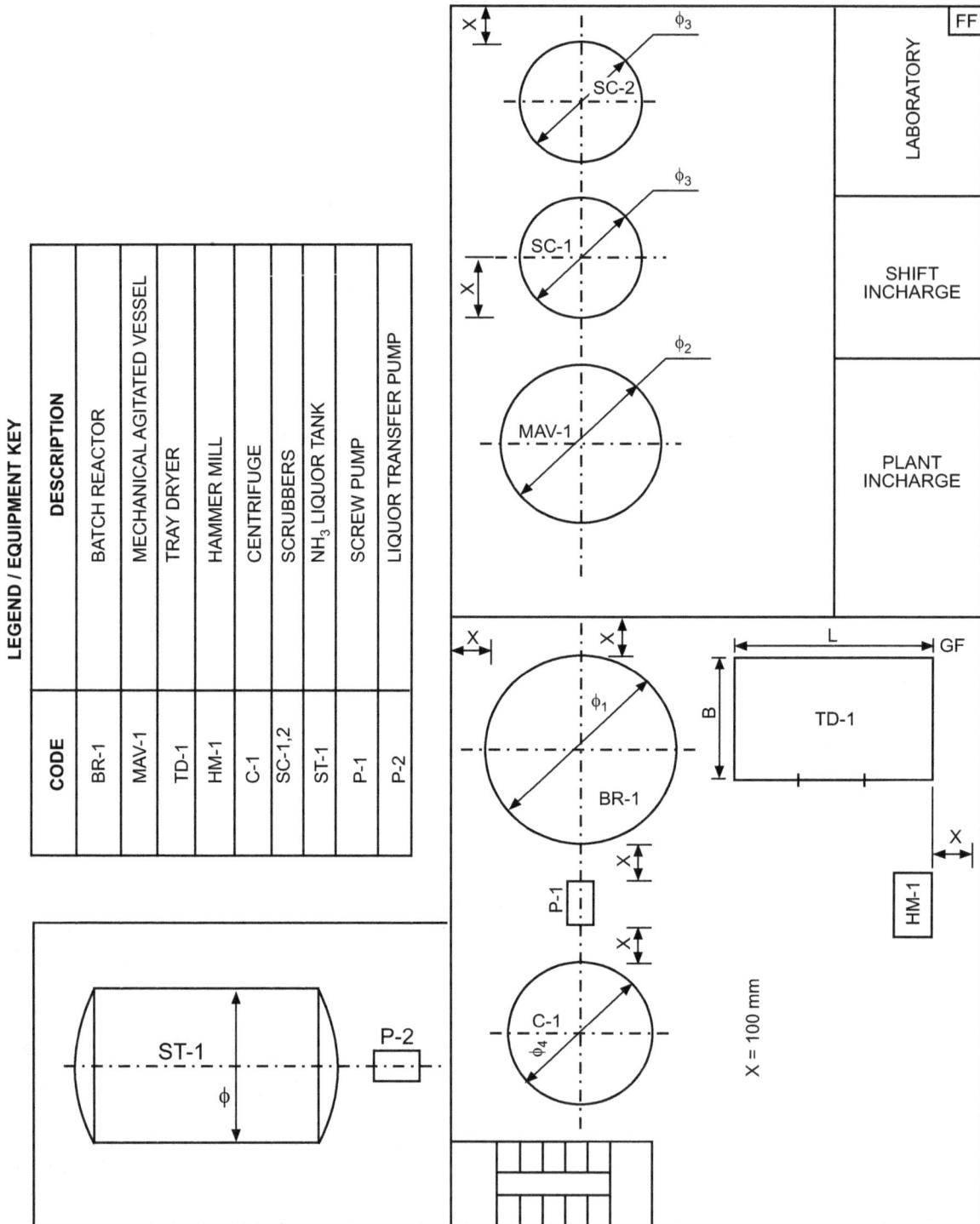

LEGEND / EQUIPMENT KEY

CODE	DESCRIPTION
BR-1	BATCH REACTOR
MAV-1	MECHANICAL AGITATED VESSEL
TD-1	TRAY DRYER
HM-1	HAMMER MILL
C-1	CENTRIFUGE
SC-1,2	SCRUBBERS
ST-1	NH_3 LIQUOR TANK
P-1	SCREW PUMP
P-2	LIQUOR TRANSFER PUMP

$X = 100$ mm

FIG. 7.54 : EQUIPMENT LAYOUT OF ONA PLANT

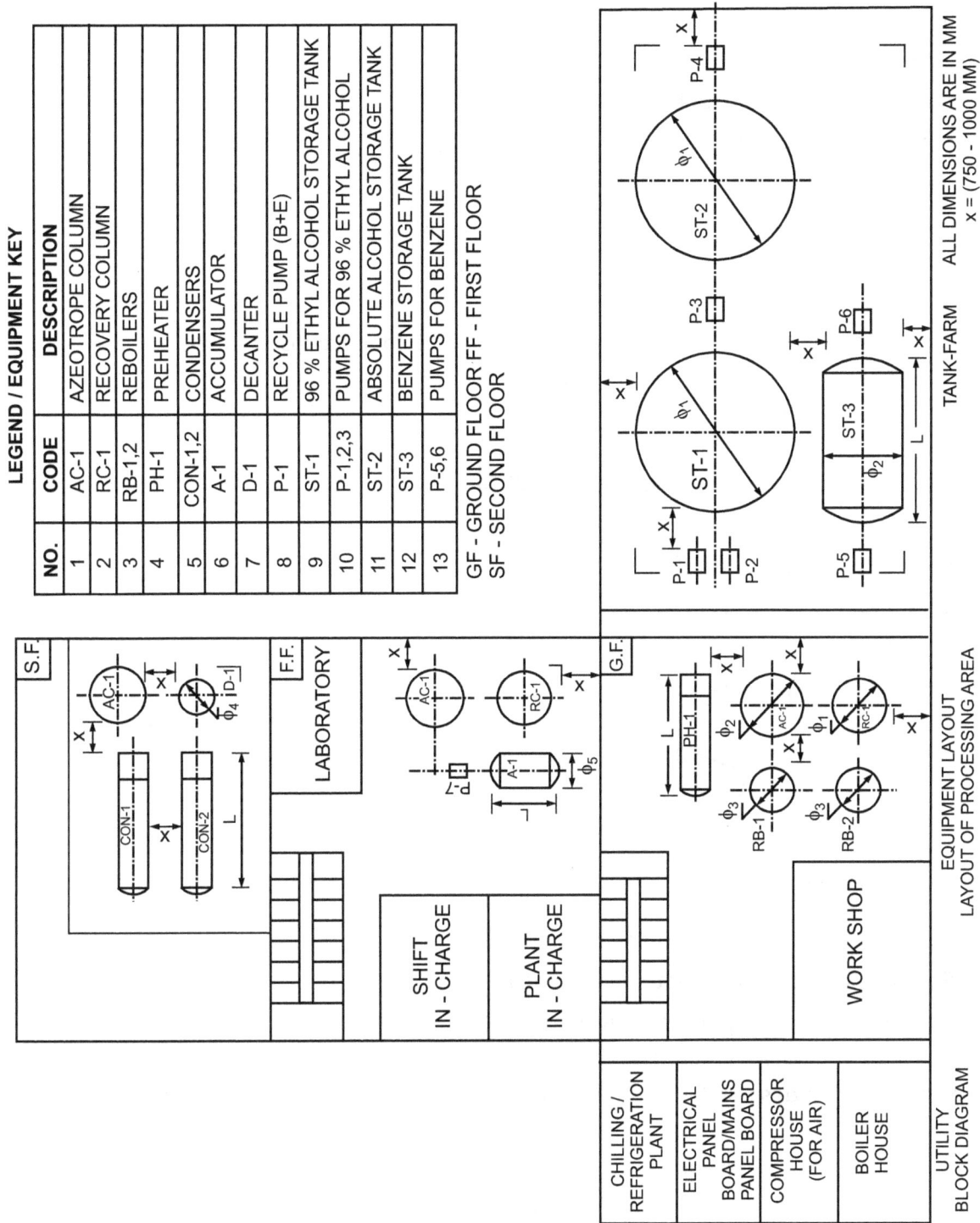

FIG. 7.55 : EQUIPMENT LAYOUT, TANK FARM, AND UBD OF ALCOHOL PLANT

7.5 DRAWING FLOW SHEET BY USING AUTO CAD

Creating objects using Auto CAD 2000 :

We can choose an object either from the draw menu or draw tool bar.

1. To draw a line :

    (i) From the Draw menu, choose line

(ii)   Specify the start point (1).

(iii)   Specify the end point (2).

(iv)   Specify the end points of the next segments (3, 4, 5).

(v)   Press Enter to complete the line.

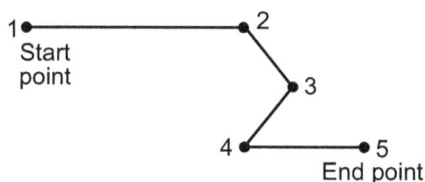

We can make use of this tool bar to show input and output connections, symbols for coil, agitator and other equipments which can be drawn by making use of line tool bar.

2.   To draw an inscribed square :

(i)   From the Draw menu, choose polygon

(ii)   Enter 4 to specify four sides of polygon.

(iii)   Specify the center point of the polygon (1).

(iv)   Enter i for inscribed in circle.

(v)   Specify the radius.

Related rectangles create polyline rectangles.

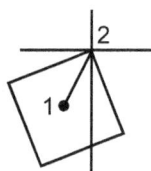

3.   To draw a rectangle :

(i)   From the Draw menu, choose rectangle

(ii)   Specify the first corner point-specify a point (1).

(iii)   Specify other corner point-specify a point (2).

The two specified points determine the diagonal corners of a rectangle with sides parallel to X and Y axes of the current UCS.

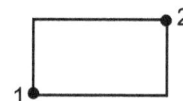

4.   To draw a circumscribed hexagon :

(i)   From the Draw menu, choose polygon

(ii)   Enter 6 for the number of sides.

(iii)   Specify the center point of the polygon (1).

(iv)   Enter C for circumscribed about the circle.

(v)   Specify the radius (2).

5.   To draw a circle by specifying a center point and radius :

(i)   From the Draw menu, choose circle ➤ center, radius

(ii)   Specify the center point.

(iii) Specify the radius.

We can also draw circle by entering other options such as 2P – 2 point method or 3P – 3 point method, i.e., by specifying two or three points lying on the circumference of a circle.

6.   To draw an arc by specifying three points :

(i)   From the Draw menu, choose arc ➤ start, center, end

(ii)   Specify the start point (1) by entering end p and selecting line.

       The arc snaps to the end point of the line.

(iii) Specify the second point (2) by entering cen and selecting the existing arc to define the center of the arc.

(iv)   Specify the end point of the arc.

Start (1), center (2),
end (3)

Center (1), start (2),
end (3)

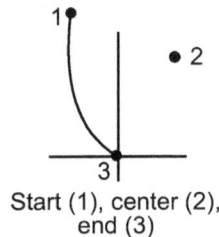

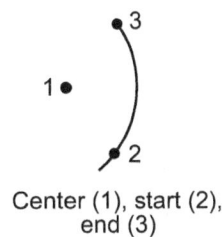

7.   To draw an arc using a start point, a center point, and a chord length :

(i)   From the Draw menu, choose arc ➤ start, center, length.

(ii)   Specify the start point (1).

(iii) Specify the center point (2).

(iv)   Specify the chord length.

8.   To draw a true ellipse using end points and distance :

(i)   From the Draw menu, choose ellipse ➤ axis, end

(ii)   Specify the first end point of the first axis (1).

(iii) Specify the second end point of the first axis (2).

(iv)   Drag the pointing device away from the mid point (3) of the first axis and click to specify the distance.

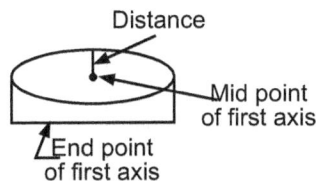

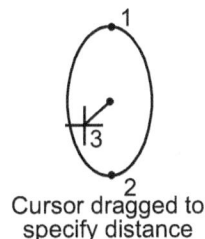

Distance

Mid point
of first axis

End point
of first axis

Cursor dragged to
specify distance

9.   To draw an elliptical arc using start and end angles :

(i)   From the Draw menu, choose ellipse ➤ arc

(ii)   Specify end points of the first axis (1 and 2).

(iii)   Specify the distance of the second axis (3).

(iv)   Specify the start angle (4).

(v)   Specify the end angle (5).

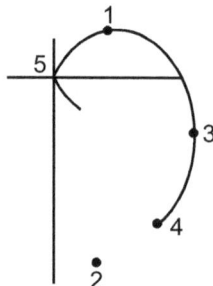

Drawing an Arrow :

In the flowsheet, we have to indicate input and output streams to and from equipments with the help of arrows.

(i)   From the pull down menu of Draw menu, select Pline (Polyline).

(ii)   Specify the first point (as per requirement) by clicking left bottom of the mouse.

(iii)   Enter w for width.

(iv)   Press Enter.

(v)   Specify starting width of an arrow, say for example enter/type 4.

(vi)   Press Enter.

(vii)   Specify ending width of an arrow - say zero - enter zero value.

(viii) Move the cursor upto the end point of an arrow as per the requirement.

(ix)   Press Enter and click left bottom of mouse. The arrow of required size will appear.

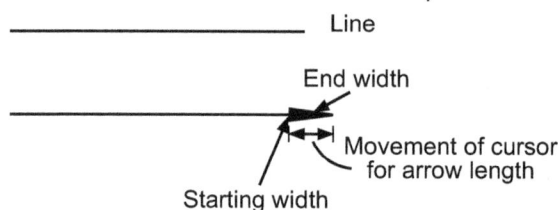

Adding Text :

(i)   From the pull down menu of Draw menu, select Text and then Multiline Text.

(ii)   Select first corner (starting point of text).

(iii)   Specify opposite corner (by clicking).

(iv)   Multiline Text Editor (MTE) appears.

(v)   In MTE enter font type, font height (value say 5).

(vi)   Press Enter.

(vii)   In MTE dialog box-type the text and click OK. The text will appear at the required location.

With single line text, we can add text at any location as per the requirements by simply moving cursor and clicking after completing the text at one location.

(i) From the pull down of the Draw menu, select text and then single line text.

(ii) Specify start point of text (by clicking).

(iii) Specify height–enter value say 7 and press Enter.

(iv) Specify rotation angle say zero degree (default value) and press Enter (for adding text on horizontal line).

For adding a text on a vertical line (that can be read from the RHS bottom corner of the paper), specify the rotation angle of 90°.

(v) Enter text ABC ... and press Enter.

(vi) Choose next location where you want to add the text by moving cursor to that location and clicking. Then enter text.

☐ Making use of MOVE command :

One can make use of MOVE command (modified tool) for moving an object (e.g., line, title block, legend block, etc.) from one location to another as per our requirement.

(i) Select MOVE from the modify tool bar.

(ii) Select an object (s) by clicking left bottom of the mouse.

(iii) Press Enter.

(iv) Specify base point (by moving cursor to that point and clicking).

(v) Move cursor to move object at desired location and click left bottom of mouse.

(vi) Press Enter for Move command to be on again.

(vii) While moving block, we have to select the entire block in single clicking.

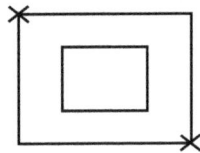

Before selecting   After selecting

☐ Array :

With the help of array command, we can make tables for tabulating data.

(i) Draw a horizontal line with ortho mode on.

(ii) Select Array command from modified tool bar.

(iii) Select line and press Enter.

(iv) Enter array type – say R (for rectangular array) and press Enter.

(v) Enter number of rows, say 5 and press Enter.

(vi) Enter number of columns, say 0 (NIL) and press Enter.

(vii) Enter distance between rows, say 10 and press Enter. The array will appear.

(viii) If a number of columns are given then we have to enter distance between the columns.

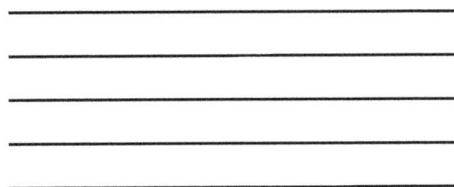

For making columns at the required distance, draw a vertical line and make use of offset command for completing the required table.

Offset command :

(i)   Select offset command from modified tool bar.

(ii)   Specify offset distance, say 10 and press Enter.

(iii)   Select object (vertical line) to offset.

(iv)   Specify point on side to offset by the moving cursor on that side and clicking left bottom of the mouse.

(v)   Press Enter to activate again offset command and repeat the procedure.

By giving variable offset distance, we can make columns of different sizes.

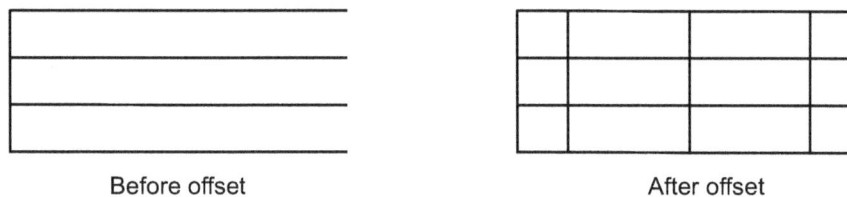

| Before offset | After offset |

Trim :

We can trim an unwanted portion of the object by making use of this tool.

(i)   Select Trim from modified tool bar.

(ii)   Select cutting edges by clicking left bottom and press Enter.

(iii)   Select object to trim - by selecting it by clicking left bottom on it, it will be trimmed.

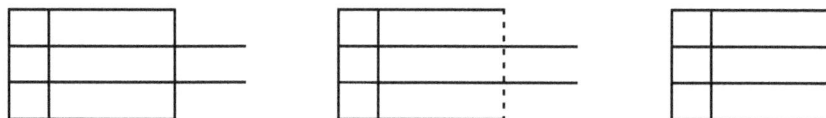

Display Commands of AutoCAD

Different AutoCAD Display commands are used to display the drawn object in the required manner.

Various display commands are :

(i)   Zoom, (ii) Pan, (iii) Redraw, (iv) Regen, etc.

Zoom :

This command increases or decreases the apparent size of the object in the current view-port. AutoCAD zoom options are used to increase or decrease the size of the image displayed in the drawing area. Zooming does not change the absolute size of the drawing but it changes the size of the view within the drawing area.

Magnifying the image to view the details more closely is called zooming in. Shrinking to see the larger portion of the time is called zooming out.

Different options of zoom command are – All, Dynamic, center, previous, etc.

Using Zoom Real time, you can zoom in or out of the drawing by moving the cursor vertically up or down.

To zoom in real time :

(i)   From view menu, choose zoom   real time.

(ii)   For zooming in or out to different magnifications, hold down the pick up botton on your pointing device and move the cursor vertically. Move the cursor above the midpoint of the drawing area to zoom in on the image. To zoom out from the image, move the cursor below the midpoint of the drawing area.

Zoom All : It zooms to display the entire drawing in the current viewport. The display shows all objects even though the drawing extents outside the drawing limits.

Zoom Center : It zooms to display a window defined by center point and magnification value or height. A smaller value for height increases magnification and vice versa.

To center drawing in the drawing area,

(i)　　From the View menu, choose zoom ➤ center.

(ii)　　Specify the point that you want in the center of the drawing.

(iii)　　Enter the height in drawing units or enter a scale factor.

Zoom Extents : It zooms to display the drawing extents and will show whatever is drawn with magnification or enlargement upto the full screen.

Zoom Dynamic : It displays the generated portion of your drawing in a viewbox.

To Zoom Dynamically :

(i)　　From the View menu, choose Zoom ➤ Dynamic.

(ii)　　When the viewbox contains an X, drag a viewbox around the screen to pan to a different area.

(iii)　　Press the pick up button on your pointing device to zoom to a different magnification. The X in the viewbox changes to an arrow.

(iv)　　Resize the viewbox by dragging the boarder to the right or left. A larger box displays the smaller image and a smaller box displays the larger image.

Zoom Window :

It is used to zoom in on an area specifying its boundaries :

(i)　　From the View menu, choose Zoom ➤　Window.

(ii)　　Specify one corner of the area you want to view.

(iii)　　Specify the opposite corner of the area you want to view.

The object present in the window box fully appears on the screen.

Zoom Previous :

To return quickly to the prior view, one can make use of this command. AutoCAD can restore upto ten previous views in succession.

To restore the previous view :

(i)　　From the View menu, choose Zoom　　➤ Previous.

Pan :

It moves the drawing display in the current viewport. It is used to shift the view of the drawing without changing the magnification. Panning is nothing but moving the screen images from one location to another.

Command line : Pan :

Realtime is the default setting for Pan. Press Enter after entering pan on the command line to automatically place you in realtime pan mode.

Hold down the pick button on the pointing device and move the hand cursor to pan the drawing.

To Pan in Realtime :

(i)　　From the View menu, choose Pan ➤　Realtime.

(ii)　　Hold down the pick button and move the pointing device to reposition the drawing.

Redraw : It refreshes the display in the current viewport. You can refresh the display to remove blips or temporary markers that indicate the points you have specified. You can use either Redraw or Regenerate to refresh the display. Redraw removes marker blips.

To Redraw the screen

From the View menu, choose Redraw

Command line : Redraw

Regen : It regenerates the entire drawing and refreshes the current viewport.
It regenerates the entire drawing and recomputes the screen coordinates for all objects.

Because regeneration can take a long time in complex drawing you usually use redraw. Redrawing cleans up only the display. Regeneration not only cleans up the display but also updates the drawing database with screen coordinates for all objects in the drawing.

To regenerate the drawing :

•   From the View menu, choose Regen.

Redo : It reverses the effect of previous undo or U command.

Redo reverses the effect of single Undo or U command. Redo must immediately follow the U or undo command.

Command line : Redo.

For drawing a flow sheet using AutoCAD, we have to make use of various draw tool bars and modified tool bars such as line, circle, arc, rectangle, text, trim, move, etc.

As it is not necessary to draw the flow sheet to the scale, we can draw the flow sheet symbols of proportionate size by selecting the required tool(s) and by moving the pointing device and clicking.

A single flow sheet symbol may require use of more than one draw tool bar. For example, drawing of the flow sheet symbol of a packed column requires use of draw tool bar either of line or rectangle and of arc.

1.   To draw a line horizontal or vertical after choosing/selecting line from draw tool bar, specify the first point (by clicking) and then move the pointing device to draw a line of required length, click to specify the end point, then right click and select enter to get the required line.

2.   To draw flow sheet symbols for coil of any type, agitator, centrifuge, inflow/out-flow arrow, etc. make use of draw tool bar of line.

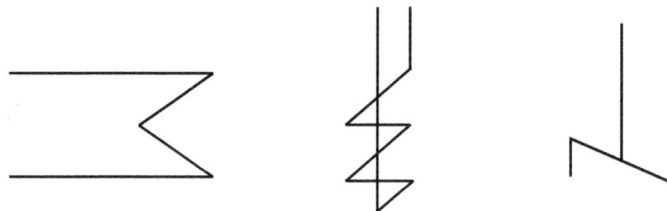

Specify first point, next points and end point.

3.   To draw a rectangle of a flow sheet symbol for plate/packed column, tray dryer, horizontal tank, etc. choose/select draw tool bar for rectangle, i.e., choose rectangle from draw tool bar, move the pointing device to required location, click to specify the first corner, drag the pointing device to draw a rectangle of required size and orientation and click to specify the opposite corner.

4.   To draw a flow sheet symbol for packed column make use of draw tool bars for rectangle, line and arc.

First draw a rectangle by choosing rectangle from draw tool bar. Then draw cross lines and horizontal lines (required) by choosing line from draw tool bar.

To draw an arc representing the top and bottom dished heads choose arc from draw tool bar, specify the first point, second point on an arc and end point of an arc by clicking [specify first point, move pointing device for cursor to be at required location and then drag/move pointing device further and specify end point to get the required arc].

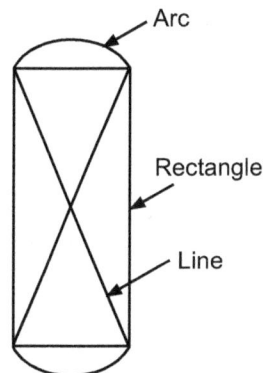

If arc extends the rectangle we can select the extended portion of an arc and erase it with erase command (from modified tool bar).

5.   To draw circle choose circle from draw tool bar, move pointing device to required location, specify the center, drag the pointing device to move the cursor away from the center and click to get a circle of required size. Always make use of a draw tool bar for drawing required flow sheet symbols.

6.   To draw a process flow sheet symbol for heat exchanger, thermosyphon type reboiler, etc. make use of draw tool bar for circle and line. Draw arrows at the end by making use of command for polyline.

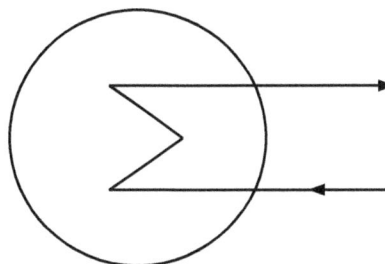

In this way we can generate flow sheet symbols for equipments involved by making use of AutoCAD 2000 and then one can draw the required flow sheet.

□□□

www.ingramcontent.com/pod-product-compliance
Lightning Source LLC
Chambersburg PA
CBHW080519090426
42734CB00015B/3106